10 Minute Guide to WordPerfect® 6.0

Joe Kraynak

alpha
books

A Division of Prentice Hall Computer Publishing

11711 North College Avenue, Carmel, Indiana 46032 USA

To my kids, Nick and Ali, for making me laugh.

International Standard Book Number: 1-56761-021-8
Library of Congress Catalog Card Number: 92-75159

96 95 94 93   8 7 6 5 4 3 2 1

Interpretation of the printing code: the rightmost double-digit number is the year of the book's printing; the rightmost single-digit number is the number of the book's printing. For example, a printing code of 93-1 shows that the first printing of the book was in 1993.

Screen reproductions in this book were created by means of the program Collage Plus from Inner Media, Inc., Hollis, NH.

Special thanks to Kelly Oliver for ensuring the technical accuracy of this book.

Printed in the United States of America

Publisher: Marie Butler-Knight
Associate Publisher: Lisa Bucki
Managing Editor: Elizabeth Keaffaber
Acquisitions Manager: Stephen R. Poland
Development Editor: Faithe Wempen
Manuscript Editor: Albright Communications, Inc.
Book Designer: Roger Morgan
Indexer: Jeanne Clark
Production: Diana Bigham, Katy Bodenmiller, Scott Cook, Tim Cox, Mark Enochs, Linda Koopman, Tom Loveman, Roger Morgan, Joe Ramon, Carrie Roth, Greg Simsic

Contents

Trademarks

All terms mentioned in this book that are known to be trademarks or service marks are listed below. In addition, terms suspected of being trademarks or service marks have been appropriately capitalized. Alpha Books cannot attest to the accuracy of this information. Use of a term in this book should not be regarded as affecting the validity of any trademark or service mark.

WordPerfect is a registered trademark of WordPerfect Corporation.

MS-DOS is a registered trademark of Microsoft Corporation.

Introduction

Congratulations! You have the most powerful word-processing program on the market—WordPerfect 6.0. With it, you can type and print a simple letter, check for errors in spelling and grammar, create your own newsletter (complete with fancy type and pieces of clipart), and do much much more. That's the good news. The bad news is that you have to learn the basics before you can even hope to get anything done.

Now What?

You could wade through the manual that came with WordPerfect to find out how to perform a specific task, but that may take a while and it may tell you more than you want to know. You need a practical guide, one that tells you exactly how to create, edit, format, and print a document.

Welcome to the *10 Minute Guide to WordPerfect 6.0*

Because most people don't have the luxury of sitting down uninterrupted for hours at a time to learn WordPerfect, this *10 Minute Guide* does not attempt to teach *everything* about the program. Instead, it focuses on the most often-used features. Each feature is covered in a single self-contained lesson, which is designed to take 10 minutes or less to complete.

The *10 Minute Guide* teaches you about the program without relying on technical jargon. With straightforward, easy-to-follow explanations and numbered lists that tell you what keys to press and what options to select, the *10 Minute Guide to WordPerfect 6.0* makes learning the program quick and easy.

Who Should Use the *10 Minute Guide to WordPerfect 6.0?*

The *10 Minute Guide to WordPerfect 6.0* is for anyone who

- Needs to learn WordPerfect 6.0 quickly

- Feels overwhelmed or intimidated by the complexity of WordPerfect

- Wants to find out quickly whether WordPerfect 6.0 meets his or her word processing needs

- Wants a clear, concise guide to the most important features of WordPerfect 6.0

How to Use This Book

The *10 Minute Guide to WordPerfect 6.0* consists of a series of lessons ranging from basic startup to a few more advanced features. If this is your first encounter with WordPerfect 6.0, you should probably work through lessons 1 through 6 in order. These lessons lead you through the process of creating, editing, and saving your documents. Subsequent lessons tell you how to use the more advanced features to search and replace text, check for spelling and grammatical errors, style the text, set the line spacing and margins, and print your document.

Icons and Conventions Used in This Book

The following icons have been added throughout the book to help you find your way around:

Timesaver Tip icons offer shortcuts and hints for using the program efficiently.

Plain English icons define new terms.

Panic Button icons appear where new users often run into trouble.

The following conventions have been used to clarify the steps you must perform:

On-screen text	Any text that appears on-screen is shown in a special type called monospace.
What you type	The information you type appears in bold color monospace.
Menu Names	The names of menus, commands, buttons, and dialog boxes are shown with the first letter capitalized for easy recognition.
Option selections	You can select many WordPerfect options by using your mouse or by typing the underlined letter in the option's name. In this book, the bolded letter corresponds to the underlined letter you see on-screen.
Key+Key Combinations	In many cases, you must press a two-key key combination in order to enter a command—for example, "Press Ctrl+X." In such cases, hold down the first key and press the second key.

For Further Reference

To learn more about WordPerfect 6.0, look for this slightly more advanced book, also by Alpha Books: *The First Book of WordPerfect 6.0*, by Kate Miller.

Lesson 1

Starting and Exiting WordPerfect

In this lesson, you learn how to start and end a typical WordPerfect work session and how to get on-line help.

Starting WordPerfect

Before you can use WordPerfect to type a document, you must start WordPerfect by performing the following steps:

1. Type wp at the DOS prompt. (If your computer has extended or expanded memory, type wp /r to tell WordPerfect to use that memory.)

2. Press Enter. The WordPerfect opening screen appears for a moment, and then the edit screen appears, as shown in Figure 1.1.

> **Extended and expanded memory.** Most new computers come with 1M of conventional memory, over half of which most programs can use directly. Memory can be added to a computer in the form of extended or expanded memory. If you are unsure whether your computer has additional memory, try the /r switch. If no additional memory is available, WordPerfect displays a message telling you so.

Bad command or filename. If you enter the WP command and you see the Bad command or filename message on-screen, you must change to the WordPerfect directory before entering the command. For example, if you installed WordPerfect in C:\WP60, type **c:** and press Enter, and then type **cd\wp60** and press Enter. Now, perform steps 1 and 2 above.

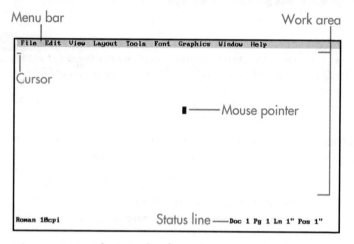

Menu bar

Work area

Cursor

Mouse pointer

Roman 18cpi   Status line ——Doc 1 Pg 1 Ln 1" Pos 1"

Figure 1.1 The WordPerfect edit screen is where you start.

Parts of the WordPerfect Screen

As shown in Figure 1.1, the WordPerfect edit screen consists of the following parts:

Menu bar. The menu bar at the top of the screen contains the names of the menus you can open. You learn how to open these menus in Lesson 2.

Cursor. The small, blinking horizontal line in the upper left of the screen is the cursor. Whatever you type is inserted at the cursor.

Work area. The main part of the screen is the work area. This is where you type your text.

Status line. The status line at the bottom of the screen provides information about the location of the cursor. The status line may also display information that tells you what you can do next.

Mouse pointer. If a mouse is installed on your computer, the mouse pointer appears on-screen as a rectangle.

> **Fast help.** If you run into trouble and cannot figure out what to do, look at the left end of the status line. This line often contains valuable information.

Getting Help

Although the status line often contains the information you need to get out of trouble, there may be times when you need more help. To get more help, open the **Help** menu by performing these steps:

1. Move the mouse pointer over **Help** in the menu bar, and then press and release the left mouse button, or press Alt+H. The **Help** menu opens as shown in Figure 1.2.

2. Choose the help option you want by typing the highlighted letter in the option's name or by clicking on the option:

   Contents. Selecting this option displays a list of general help categories. Use the arrow keys to highlight a category and press Enter or click on the desired category.

   Index. The Index option displays an alphabetical list of help topics, as shown in Figure 1.3. Use the arrow keys to highlight a topic and press Enter, or click on the desired topic.

How Do I. The How Do I option takes a more practical view of help topics. It groups the help topics in logical categories, such as Basic Layout and Macros, and lists the topics in a way in which you are likely to ask for help—for example, "How do I save a document?"

Coaches. Coaches are on-line tutors that lead you through the process of performing a given task.

Macros. The Macros option provides a list of help topics specifically for creating macros.

Tutorial. The Tutorial option allows you to work through several lessons that teach you the WordPerfect basics.

WP Info. This option displays some general information about the WordPerfect program. If you entered your registration number the first time you ran WordPerfect, the information screen also displays this number.

What's a macro? A macro is a collection of recorded keystrokes or menu selections that you can play back simply by pressing a key combination or by selecting the macro from a menu. You can record dozens of keystrokes in a macro and play them back simply by pressing two keys.

Context-sensitive help. To get help for a task you are currently trying to perform, start performing the task until you get to the point at which you need help. Then, press the F1 key.

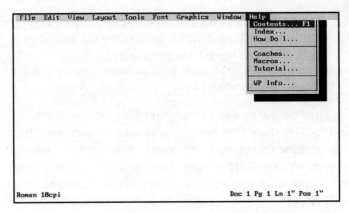

Figure 1.2 The **H**elp menu contains several help options.

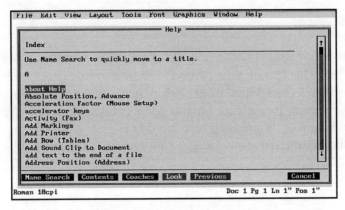

Figure 1.3 Select the desired topic from the help index.

Exiting WordPerfect

When you are finished working in WordPerfect, you can exit the program by performing the following steps:

1. Move the mouse pointer over **F**ile in the menu bar, and then press and release the left mouse button, or press Alt+F. The **F**ile menu opens.

2. Type X to select Exit WP. WordPerfect displays a
       dialog box asking if you want to save the file; skip
       to Lesson 6 to learn how to save a file.

3. Press Enter to select Exit.

The File menu also has another Exit option. If you
select Exit, you are first asked if you want to save your file
before exiting the current document. You are then asked if
you want to exit WordPerfect. This option is useful if you
want to quit working on a document but you want to stay in
WordPerfect.

> **Quick exit.** To exit with the keyboard, press
> and release the Home key and then press the F7
> key.

In this lesson, you learned how to start and exit
WordPerfect and how to get help when you need it. In the
next lesson, you'll learn how to enter commands in
WordPerfect by pressing command keys and selecting
options from menus.

Lesson 2

Entering Commands in WordPerfect

In this lesson, you learn how to enter commands in WordPerfect by using the pull-down menus, shortcut keys, and dialog boxes.

Selecting Commands from the Menu Bar

At the top of the WordPerfect screen is the menu bar, which contains the names of the menus you can open. Each menu contains several related options. Table 2.1 provides a general overview of the pull-down menus.

Table 2.1 WordPerfect's pull-down menus.

Menu name	Options
File	Contains file-oriented commands including commands for opening, exiting, saving, and printing documents.
Edit	Includes commands for cutting, pasting, and copying text, and undoing your changes, and for searching for and replacing text.
View	Includes commands for changing the display from Text to Graphics mode, and for turning various screen features (such as the menu bar and button bar) on and off.

continues

Table 2.1 Continued.

Menu name	Options
Layout	Allows you to control the look of your document, including the margins, indents, and tab settings.
Tools	Includes writing tools, such as the spell checker and thesaurus, an indexing tool, and tables.
Font	Contains options for enhancing your text and selecting a different type size or design.
Graphics	Includes options for pulling illustrations and clip art into your documents and for adding lines, boxes, and borders.
Window	Allows you to change from window to window and arrange the windows on-screen so that you can work on more than one document at a time (see Lesson 23).
Help	Lets you access various Help features.

Figure 2.1 shows the menu bar with the File menu pulled down. Note that some options are followed by a right-pointing arrow and other options are followed by an ellipsis (...). Selecting an option followed by a right arrow pens a submenu which presents a list of additional options. Selecting an option with an ellipsis displays a dialog box which prompts you to enter more information, as explained later in this lesson.

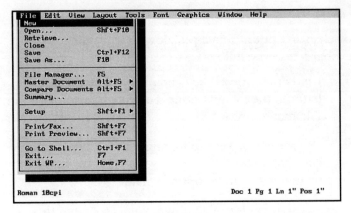

File Edit View Layout Tools Font Graphics Window Help
New
Open...   Shft+F10
Retrieve...
Close
Save   Ctrl+F12
Save As...   F10

File Manager...   F5
Master Document   Alt+F5   ▶
Compare Documents   Alt+F5   ▶
Summary...

Setup   Shft+F1 ▶

Print/Fax...   Shft+F7
Print Preview...   Shft+F7

Go to Shell...   Ctrl+F1
Exit...   F7
Exit WP...   Home,F7

Roman 10cpi   Doc 1 Pg 1 Ln 1" Pos 1"

Figure 2.1   A pull-down menu presents a list of options.

Lost menu bar? If the menu bar is not displayed, press Alt+= or click the right mouse
button. To have the menu bar displayed permanently, type **V** to open the **V**iew menu and then
type **P** to select **P**ull-Down Menus.

Using Your Mouse

To select an option from a pull-down menu using your
mouse, take the following steps:

1. Move the mouse pointer over the name of the menu
   you want to pull down, and click the left mouse
   button.

2. Click on the desired option in the menu.

Escape. To close the menu without entering a
command, click anywhere outside the menu.

Using Your Keyboard

To select an option from a pull-down menu using your keyboard, take the following steps:

1. Hold down the Alt key and press the highlighted letter in the menu's name. For example, to open the File menu, press Alt+F.

2. Use the arrow keys to highlight the desired option, and then press the Enter key, or press the highlighted letter in the option's name.

Once a menu is pulled down, you can switch to a different menu by pressing ← or →. The current menu is then closed, and the menu to the left or right is opened.

> **Escape.** To close the menu without entering a command, press the Esc key twice. The first time you press Esc, the menu is closed, but the menu bar remains active. When you press Esc the second time, you deactivate the menu bar.

Using Shortcut Keys

In Figure 2.1, notice that some of the options on the **File** menu have corresponding keystrokes. For example, the **Print/Fax** command has the keystroke Shift+F7. Instead of opening the menu and then selecting **Print/Fax**, you can simply hold down the Shift key while pressing the F7 key. For a list of shortcut keys, refer to the inside back cover of this book.

Responding to Dialog Boxes

Many options on the pull-down menus display a dialog box when selected. For example, if you select the **Print/Fax** command from the File menu, you see the Print/Fax dialog box, as shown in Figure 2.2. Dialog boxes contain one or more of the following elements:

Option buttons. You can select only one option button in a group of option buttons. When you select one button it deactivates the other button.

Check box options. When you select an option, an X appears in the checkbox, indicating that the option is selected. To turn the option off, select it again. You can select more than one option in a group.

List boxes. A list box contains several items from which you can select. (List boxes are not shown in Figure 2.2.)

Drop-down list boxes. Like list boxes, a drop-down list box contains several items from which to choose. However, only one item in the list is initially displayed. To see the rest of the items, you must pull down the list.

Text boxes. A text box allows you to type specific information, such as the name of a file. If the text box contains text, you can replace it by typing new text. To edit an entry, click inside the text box or use ← or → to move the cursor. Then use the Del key to delete single characters, and type your change.

Command buttons. Most dialog boxes contain at least two command buttons: one for executing the command, and one for canceling it.

Additional dialog boxes. Some options in a dialog box may be followed by ellipses. Selecting one of these options opens another dialog box. Once you enter your preferences in the second dialog box, you are returned to the first one.

Option buttons   Check box option   Command button / Text box

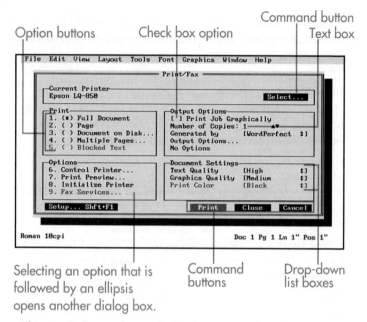

Selecting an option that is followed by an ellipsis opens another dialog box.

Command buttons

Drop-down list boxes

Figure 2.2 With any dialog box, you select the desired options and then press a command button to execute the command.

Using Your Mouse

To move around in a dialog box with the mouse, click on the desired option, item, or button. Clicking on an option button or a check box toggles the setting on or off. Clicking on the arrow to the right of a drop-down list pulls down the list. Clicking inside a text box allows you to edit its contents. Clicking on a command button closes the dialog box and executes the command.

Using Your Keyboard

The easiest way to select a dialog box option with the keyboard is to type the option's number or the highlighted letter in the option's name. Another way to select an option is to use the Tab key or arrow keys to highlight the option and then press Enter.

In this lesson, you learned how to enter commands in WordPerfect by using pull-down menus, dialog boxes, and shortcut keys. In the next lesson, you learn how to change the look and feel of WordPerfect to make it easier to use.

Lesson 3
Making WordPerfect Easier to Use

In this lesson, you learn how to switch from text mode to graphics mode, how to turn on the WordPerfect button bar, and how to turn on a ribbon for quick text and document formatting.

Changing Display Modes

One of the niftiest new features introduced in WordPerfect 6 is the WYSIWYG (what-you-see-is-what-you-get) feature. Turn on graphics mode, and you can see how the text (and any graphic elements you add later) will appear in print. You also see better-looking menus, dialog boxes, and other elements that make WordPerfect easier to use.

To change to graphics mode, perform the following steps:

1. Press Alt+V or click on View in the menu bar.

2. Type G or click on Graphics Mode. WordPerfect switches to graphics mode, as shown in Figure 3.1.

Not enough memory for Graphics mode? WordPerfect uses more of your computer's memory to run in Graphics mode. If your computer seems too slow in Graphics mode or you start getting messages that tell you there is not enough memory to perform a specific task, switch back to text mode (select **V**iew/**T**ext Mode).

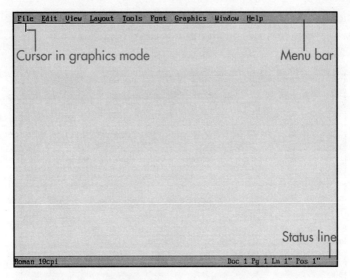

File Edit View Layout Tools Font Graphics Window Help

Cursor in graphics mode   Menu bar

                                                     Status line

Roman 10cpi   Doc 1 Pg 1 Ln 1" Pos 1"

Figure 3.1 WordPerfect in Graphics mode.

Using the Button Bar

WordPerfect 6 comes with a button bar that you can use
(with a mouse) to quickly enter commonly used commands.
To turn the button bar on or off, perform the following
steps:

1. Press Alt+V or click on View in the menu bar.

2. Type B or click on Button Bar. The button bar
appears just below the menu bar, as shown in
Figure 3.2.

To enter a command using the button bar, use your
mouse to click on the button for the command you want to
enter.

Turning On the Formatting Ribbon

In addition to the button bar, you can turn on a formatting
ribbon that allows you to change the look of your text

quickly. For example, you can use the ribbon to change the size of your text or the alignment (left, right, or center).

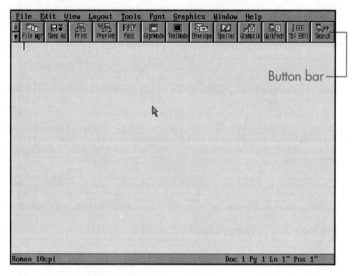

Figure 3.2 The button bar allows you to perform tasks simply by clicking on a button.

Formatting. When you create a document, you typically work on two aspects of the document: its content and format. The content is the text you type. The format is the look and layout of the text. Formatting includes changing the margins, line spacing, and type size, and enhancing text with bold, italic, and underlining.

To turn the ribbon on or off, perform the following steps:

1. Press Alt+V or click on View in the menu bar.

2. Type R or click on Ribbon. The ribbon appears, between the menu bar and the button bar, as shown in Figure 3.3.

To use most options in the ribbon, move the mouse pointer over the option, hold down the left mouse button, and drag the highlight over the setting or item you want to choose. When you release the mouse button, the highlighted setting is put into effect.

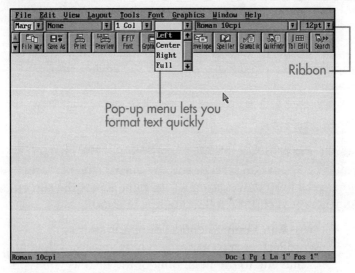

Figure 3.3 The ribbon allows you to format text quickly.

In this lesson, you learned how to control the look of WordPerfect by changing to Graphics mode and how to make WordPerfect easier to use by turning on the button bar and ribbon. In the next lesson, you learn how to start typing your document.

Lesson 4
Entering Text

In this lesson, you learn how to type text in a document and move the cursor around with the keyboard and mouse.

Typing Text

To enter text in WordPerfect, start typing. The characters you type appear on-screen, and the cursor (the blinking horizontal line) moves from left to right across the screen. As you type, keep the following tips in mind:

- Press Enter only to end a paragraph or a short line. WordPerfect automatically wraps text from the end of one line to the beginning of the next as you type (see Figure 4.1). Press Enter twice at the end of a paragraph if you want a blank line between paragraphs.

- Press the Tab key at the beginning of a paragraph to indent the first line of a paragraph 5 spaces.

- You cannot use the down arrow key to move down until you have some text to move down to. Press the Enter key to move down, essentially creating a new line.

- Any text that won't fit on the screen scrolls off the top of the screen. The text is still there; you just can't see it. You will learn how to bring this text into view later in this lesson.

Press Enter to end a paragraph
or to end a short line.

Zoom drop-down menu

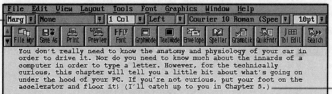

Press Enter again to leave a blank line between paragraphs.

Figure 4.1 As you type, WordPerfect wraps text from one line to the next.

Tiny text. In Graphics mode, text may appear too tiny to read. To zoom in on the text, open the **V**iew menu, select **Z**oom, and select the desired zoom percentage (150% works well). If the ribbon is displayed, use the zoom drop-down menu on the left end of the ribbon to select the zoom percentage (see Figure 4.1).

Moving Around in a Document

Once you have some text on-screen, you can start moving the cursor around inside the document. You can move the cursor using either the keyboard or the mouse, as explained in the following sections.

Using Your Keyboard

Before you can start editing your document or formatting
your text, you must know how to move around inside a
document. To move around with the keyboard, use the keys
listed in Table 4.1.

Table 4.1 Cursor-movement keys.

Press	To Move
↑	Up one line
↓	Down one line
←	One character to the left
→	One character to the right
Ctrl+→	One word to the right
Ctrl+←	One word to the left
End	To the end of the current line
Home,←*	To the left edge of the screen or the beginning of the current line
Home,→*	To the right edge of the screen or the end of the current line
Home,↓	To the bottom of the screen and then down one screenful of text
Home,↑	To the top of the screen and then up one screenful of text
PgUp	To the top of the previous page
PgDn	To the top of the next page
Home,Home,↑*	To the top of the document
Home,Home,↓*	To the bottom of the document

*When a series of keystrokes is separated by commas, press and
release each key one at a time.

Using Your Mouse

Using the mouse to move around in a document is more intuitive. To move the cursor with the mouse, perform any of the following steps:

- To move the cursor to a specific character, move the mouse pointer over the character and click the left mouse button.

- To see text that has scrolled off the top of the screen, hold down the right mouse button and drag the mouse pointer to the top of the screen. The text scrolls down into view.

- To see text that has scrolled off the bottom of the screen, hold down the right mouse button and drag the mouse pointer to the bottom of the screen. The text scrolls up into view.

Using Scroll Bars

Some users find it easier to scroll around in a document using scroll bars, as shown in Figure 4.2. The horizontal scroll bar lets you scroll text from left to right across the screen. The vertical scroll bar lets you view text that has scrolled off the top or bottom of the screen. To turn a scroll bar on or off, perform the following steps:

1. Press Alt+V or click on View in the menu bar.

2. To turn the horizontal scroll bar on or off, type H or click on Horizontal Scroll Bar.

3. To turn the vertical scroll bar on or off, type V or click on Vertical Scroll Bar.

Scroll arrow   Vertical scroll bar   Scroll box

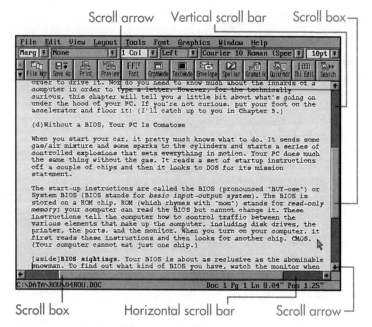

Scroll box   Horizontal scroll bar   Scroll arrow

Figure 4.2   Scroll bars can help you move around in a document.

Perform any of the following steps to use a scroll bar:

- Click on the arrow at the end of the scroll bar to scroll up, down, left, or right one line or character at a time. To scroll continuously in the direction of the arrow, hold down the mouse button.

- Drag the scroll box in the scroll bar to move to the same relative location in the document. For example, if you drag the scroll box to the middle of the scroll bar, you are in the middle of the document.

- Click twice inside the scroll bar, on either side of the scroll box, to scroll one screenful of text in the direction of the click. For example, if you click above the scroll box in the scroll bar, you move to the previous screenful of text. (When moving up or down, the first click moves the cursor to the top or bottom of the screen; the second click displays the next or previous screenful of text.)

In this lesson, you learned how to type text and how to move around inside a document. In the next lesson, you'll learn how to edit your document by adding and deleting text.

Lesson 5
Editing Text

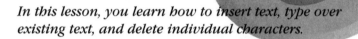

In this lesson, you learn how to insert text, type over existing text, and delete individual characters.

Inserting Text

You can insert text anywhere in a WordPerfect document. For example, you may want to insert a sentence in the middle of a paragraph or add a word to the beginning of a paragraph. To insert text, perform the following steps:

1. Move the cursor where you want the text inserted.

2. Type the text. As you type, WordPerfect moves the existing text to the right and rewraps the text.

Typing Over Existing Text

WordPerfect starts in Insert mode; whatever you type is inserted at the cursor, and existing text is moved to make room for the new text. If you want to replace text in Insert mode, you must first delete existing text and then type the new text. However, sometimes it is faster to type over existing text. To type over text, perform the following steps:

1. Move the cursor to the beginning of the text you want to type over.

2. Press the Ins key to switch from Insert to Typeover mode. Typeover appears in the left corner of the screen, as shown in Figure 5.1.

3. Start typing. Each character you type replaces an existing character on-screen.

4. When you are finished typing, press the Ins key to switch back to Insert mode. Typeover disappears from the screen.

> **Tab key behavior.** In Typeover mode, the Tab key moves from one tab stop to the next without indenting text. If you want to use the Tab key to indent the first line of a paragraph, you must change back to Insert mode.

Whatever you type starts replacing existing text from this point on.

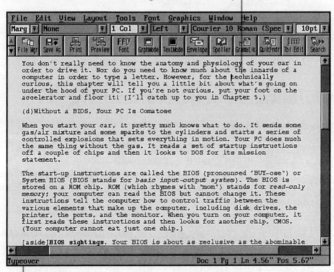

Look at the status line to see if you are in Typeover mode.

Figure 5.1 WordPerfect shows you when you are in Typeover mode.

Deleting Characters and Words

In Lessons 8 and 9, you learn how to delete blocks of text, including sentences, paragraphs, and pages. However, to make minor corrections, you can delete individual characters or words by performing any of the following steps:

• Move the cursor under the character you want to delete (or to the left of the character, in Graphics mode) and press the Del key.

• Move the cursor to the right of the character you want to delete and press the Backspace key.

• To delete a word, move the cursor under any character in the word you want to delete and press Ctrl+Backspace or Ctrl+Del.

• To delete from the cursor position to the end of a line, move the cursor to the place where you want to begin deleting and press Ctrl+End.

Undeleting Characters and Words

As you delete text, WordPerfect stores your last three deletions in a temporary holding area. You can undelete the text by performing the following steps:

1. Move the cursor where you want the undeleted text inserted.

2. Press the Esc key or open the Edit menu and select Undelete. The Undelete dialog box appears, and the most recently deleted text appears highlighted in the document, as shown in Figure 5.2.

3. To view a previous deletion, select Previous Deletion. The previously deleted text appears highlighted in the document.

4. When you see the text you want to undelete, select Restore. The text is inserted at the cursor position.

You can restore the text.   You can look at the previous deletion.

```
File   Edit   View   Layout   Tools   Font   Graphics   Window   Help
Marg [▼] None              [▼] 1 Col [▼] Left [▼] Courier 10 Roman (Spee [▼]  10pt [▼]
┌─────┬─────┬─────┬─────┐           Undelete             ┌─────┬─────┬─────┬─────┐
│File Mgr│Save As│Print│Pre│                              │GramtLik│QuikFndr│Tbl Edit│Search│
[o]   ROM (read-d─ 1. Restore                    es it
[o]   RAM (random   2. Previous Deletion          what RAM does
[o]   Where DOS c
[o]   Why your co              ┌────────┐
                               │ Cancel │
[o]   What happens when you run a program
[o]   What happens when you type information

You don't really need to know the ░anatomy and physiology░of your car in
order to drive it. Nor do you need to know much about the innards of a
computer in order to type a letter. However. for the technically
curious, this chapter will tell you a little bit about what's going on
under the hood of your PC. If you're not curious, put your foot on the
accelerator and floor it! (I'll catch up to you in Chapter 5.)

(d)Without a BIOS, Your PC Is Comatose

When you start your car, it pretty much knows what to do. It sends some
gas/air mixture and some sparks to the cylinders and starts a series of
controlled explosions that sets everything in motion. Your PC does much
the same thing without the gas. It reads a set of startup instructions
off a couple of chips and then it looks to DOS for its mission
statement.

Typeover Block on                          Doc 1 Pg 1 Ln 4.28" Pos 6"
```

The most recently deleted text appears highlighted.

Figure 5.2 You can restore the three most recent deletions.

Undeleting typed over text. If you type over text in Typeover mode, WordPerfect stores the replaced text just as if you had deleted it. You can undelete the text as explained previously.

Undoing Your Changes

You may have noticed that the Edit menu also contains an Undo command. This command undoes the previously entered command, but undoes only one command. If you accidentally delete text and immediately realize your mistake, you can restore the text by selecting Undo from the Edit menu or by pressing Ctrl+Z. WordPerfect automatically undoes the action without asking you to confirm.

In this lesson, you learned how to insert text, type over existing text, and delete and undelete characters and words. In the next lesson, you will learn how to save your document to disk.

Lesson 6

Saving and Retrieving Documents

In this lesson, you learn how to save the document you are working on to disk and open a saved document in WordPerfect.

Saving a Document to Disk

As you type, your work is saved in your computer's memory (RAM) and is erased when you quit WordPerfect (or if the power to your computer is turned off). To store your work permanently, you must save it in a named file on disk.

Naming Files

When you enter the command to save a file, WordPerfect displays a dialog box that asks you to name the file. When naming a file, follow these filename conventions:

- A filename consists of a base name (up to eight characters), a period, and an optional extension (up to three characters).

- You can use any characters in the base name and extension except the following:

  space + = | \ / < > , [ ] " : ; ? *

Specifying a Location for the File

Unless you specify otherwise, WordPerfect saves your document on the drive and directory designated in the Setup/Location of Files option (which you learn about later in this lesson). To save the file on a different drive or in a different directory, you must type a path to that directory. For example, if you wanted to save a file in the BOOKS subdirectory of the DATA directory, and name it CHPT01.WPF, you would type the following:

```
C:\DATA\BOOKS\CHPT01.WPF
```

> **Paths.** A path consists of a drive letter, a colon, and the directories that lead to the directory in which you want to save the file. The directory names are separated by a backslash (\).

Saving a Document for the First Time

When you save a document for the first time, you must assign a name to the document. Perform the following steps to save a file you have just created:

1. Open the File menu and select Save. The Save Document dialog box appears, as shown in Figure 6.1.

2. In the Filename text box, type a name for the file. (You can add a path before the filename to specify the drive and directory where you want the file saved.)

3. Press Enter or click on the OK button with your mouse. WordPerfect saves the document to disk and displays the document's location and filename in the lower left corner of the screen.

Type a name for the file.

Save Document 1	
Filename:	
Format:	WordPerfect 6.0

Setup... Shft+F1   Code Page... F9

File List... F5   QuickList... F6   Password... F8   OK   Cancel

Figure 6.1 The Save Document dialog box prompts you to name the file.

Saving a Saved Document

When you save a document, only its current contents are saved to disk. If you add or delete text or change the document in some other way, those changes are stored only in your computer's temporary memory. To prevent your changes from getting lost, you should save your document regularly to disk. To save a document that you have already named, perform one of the following steps:

- Open the File menu and select Save.

  OR

- Press Ctrl+F12.

>
> **Save As.** The Save **A**s command on the File menu lets you save a copy of the current file using a different file name. You can then edit the copy without changing the original file. Its shortcut key is F10.

Saving a Document and Clearing the Screen

To save a document and clear the screen (so you can start creating a new document), perform the following steps:

1. Press F7 or open the File menu and select Exit. A dialog box appears, asking if you want to save your changes before exiting.

2. Select Yes. Another dialog box appears, asking if you want to leave WordPerfect.

3. Press Enter or select No to remain in WordPerfect. The document is saved and the screen is cleared.

Specifying a Default Directory to Save Document Files

If you save most of the document files you create in the same directory, you can set up that directory as the default. Then, you don't have to type a path every time you save or open a file. WordPerfect saves all files in the default directory.

To specify a new default directory, you must first create the directory at the DOS prompt or from within WordPerfect (see Lesson 23). Perform the following steps to designate the new directory as the default:

1. Press Shift+F1 or open the File menu and select Setup.

2. Select Location of Files. The Location of Files dialog box appears.

3. Select Documents. The path next to the Documents option appears highlighted.

4. Type a path to the directory you want to use as the default. For example, to save all files in the DATA directory on drive C, type C:\DATA.

5. Select OK. The specified directory will now be used for all files you create and save.

6. Select Close to return to WordPerfect.

Opening or Retrieving a Document

When you save a document, it is saved in a file on disk. You can open or retrieve the file later; the document appears on-screen where you can work on it.

> **Open or retrieve?** When you open a document, WordPerfect creates a new document window for the document and retrieves the document into that window. You can then switch from one document window to another by pressing Shift+F3. When you retrieve a document, it is retrieved into the current window at the cursor position (so, you can retrieve one document into another).

Opening a Document

If you know the location and name of the file you want to open, perform the following steps to open a document file. If you do not know the name or location of the file, skip ahead to the section called "Using the File Manager to Open and Retrieve Documents."

1. Press Shift+F10 or open the File menu and select Open. The Open Document dialog box appears.

2. Type the drive letter, path, and name of the file you want to open.

3. Press Enter or click on the OK button. WordPerfect opens a new document window and retrieves the specified document into the window.

> **Starting a new document.** To open an empty document window, open the File menu and select New.

Retrieving a Document

If you know the location and name of the file you want to retrieve, perform the following steps to retrieve a document file. If you do not know the name or location of the file, skip ahead to the section called "Using the File Manager to Open and Retrieve Documents."

1. Change to the document window in which you want to retrieve the document. (Press Shift+F3 to switch document windows.)

2. Move the cursor where you want to insert the document.

3. Open the File menu and select Retrieve. The Retrieve Document dialog box appears.

4. Type the drive letter, path, and name of the file you want to retrieve.

5. Press Enter or click on the OK button. WordPerfect opens a new document window and retrieves the specified document into the window.

> **Quickly opening a file you recently worked on.** WordPerfect "remembers" the names and locations of the last four files you worked on. To open one of these files quickly, press the down arrow key when the cursor is in the Filename text box, or click on the down arrow with your mouse. The Filename list appears. Highlight the name of the file you want to open, and press Enter.

Using the File Manager to Open and Retrieve Documents

If you do not know the location or name of the document file you want to open or retrieve, use the File Manager as explained in the following steps:

1. If you want to retrieve a document, change to the desired document window by pressing Shift+F3. Move the cursor where you want the document inserted.

2. Press F5 or open the File menu and select File Manager. The Specify File Manager List dialog box appears.

3. Type a path to the directory where you think the file is located, or press F8 to view the directory tree, and then select a directory.

4. Press Enter. The File Manager appears, as shown in Figure 6.2.

5. To move to a different directory, highlight the directory and press Enter. To move up one level in the directory tree, highlight .. Parent <Dir> and press Enter. A list of files in the selected directory appears.

6. Highlight the name of the file you want to open or retrieve.

7. To open the file, select Open into New Document. To retrieve the file, select Retrieve into Current Doc.

```
▓▓▓▓▓▓▓▓▓▓▓▓▓▓▓▓▓▓ File Manager ▓▓▓▓▓▓▓▓▓▓▓▓▓▓▓▓▓▓
Directory:  C:\DATA\WP51\FILES\*.*
                                              04-05-93  04:24p
 ┌Sort by: Filename────────────────────────┐ ↑
 │ .    Current    <Dir>                    │   1. Open into New Document
 │ ..   Parent     <Dir>                    │   2. Retrieve into Current Doc
 │ ADDRESS .        3,089  01-07-92 02:27p  │   3. Look...
 │ ADDRESS .BK!     1,356  09-21-90 08:19a  │
 │ ADDRESS .SF      2,256  12-30-91 09:31a  │   4. Copy...
 │ BASEBALL.TBL     8,168  04-13-92 09:10a  │   5. Move/Rename...
 │ BINDING .WPF     4,393  11-28-90 11:19a  │   6. Delete
 │ BOOK    .WPF       987  12-30-91 09:00a  │   7. Print...
 │ BUISCARD.BK!    19,606  04-04-92 03:01p  │   8. Print List
 │ BUISCARD.WPF    10,570  04-04-92 03:11p  │
 │ BUSINESS.STY     4,096  04-02-91 10:15a  │   9. Sort by...
 │ CAPITAL .WPF    18,956  12-23-91 05:20p  │   H. Change Default Dir...
 │ CH7     .BK!    51,823  01-07-92 02:49p  │   U. Current Dir... F5
 │ CH7     .WP5    51,823  01-07-92 02:49p  │   F. Find...
 │ CHAPT2  .       57,005  12-17-91 01:59p  │   E. Search... F2
 │ CHAPT2  .DOC    51,200  08-22-90 09:43a  │   N. Name Search
 │ CHKLIST .CPS       108  02-16-93 01:49p  │
 │ CHKLIST .MS        108  11-03-92 03:54p  │   * (Un)mark
 │ CHPT04  .WPF    15,147  04-05-93 10:09a  │   Home,* (Un)mark All
 └Files:    63──────Marked:              ─┘ ↓
  Free:  15,093,760  Used:        848,222      [Setup... Shft+F1] [Close]
```

Select Parent to move up one directory in the tree.

Figure 6.2 Use the File Manager to select a file from a list of files.

More File Manager techniques. The File Manager is a powerful tool for helping you find and manage your disks, directories, and files without ever having to leave WordPerfect. For more information about using the File Manager, refer to Lesson 23.

In this lesson, you learned how to save a newly created file and save changes to a file that you have already saved to disk. You also learned how to open and retrieve saved files from disk into WordPerfect so that you can continue working on them. In the next lesson, you will learn how to preview your document before printing it and how to print a paper copy of your document.

Lesson 7

Previewing and Printing Your Document

In this lesson, you learn how to display your document as it appears in print and how to print a paper copy of your document.

Selecting a Printer

When you install WordPerfect, the Installation program asks you to select one or more printers for use with WordPerfect. If you select only one printer, you do not have to select a printer before you print. If you select more than one printer, you must select the printer you want to use by performing the following steps:

1. Press Shift+F7 or open the File menu and select Print/Fax. The Print dialog box appears.

2. Type **S** or click on the Select button. The Select Printer dialog box appears, as shown in Figure 7.1.

3. Use the arrow keys to highlight the printer you want to use and press Enter, or double-click on the name of the printer. You are returned to the Print dialog box.

4. Click on the Close button or tab to it and press Enter.

If you install more than one printer when you install WordPerfect, a list of available printers appears.

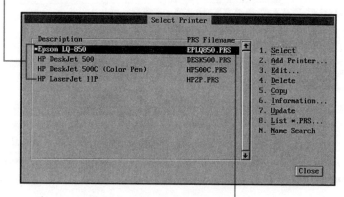

The currently selected printer is marked with an asterisk.

Figure 7.1 Use the Select Printer dialog box to choose the printer you want to use.

Previewing Your Document

It is often useful to see how your document will look in print before printing it. The Print Preview command allows you to see how the text will look on the page and how any graphic elements will appear in relation to the text. To preview your document, perform the following steps:

1. Open the File menu and select Print Preview, or click on the Preview button in the button bar. The document appears in the Print Preview screen, as shown in Figure 7.2.

2. To return to the edit screen, press F7, or open the File menu and select Close, or click on the Close button in the button bar.

Menu bar

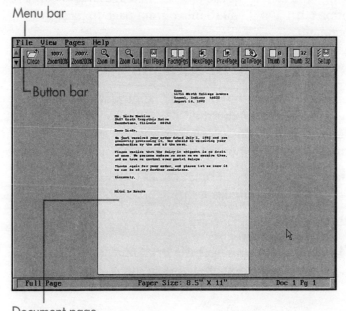

Button bar

Document page

Figure 7.2 The Print Preview screen shows how the document will appear in print.

The pull-down menus and the buttons in the button bar allow you to change the view of your document and select the pages you want to display. Most of the buttons in the button bar are self-explanatory. However, the two right buttons, Thumb 8 and Thumb 32, require some explanation; these buttons allow you to display 8 or 32 pages at the same time, giving you an overall view of a large document.

If you do not have a mouse, you can select the same
options offered in the button bar by using the pull-down
menus. The **V**iew menu contains options that allow you to
change the display of the pages. The **P**ages menu contains
options that allow you to move from page to page in a
document.

Printing Your Document

To print a document, you must first display the document in
the edit screen (not in Print Preview). Once the document is
displayed in the edit screen, perform the following steps to
print the entire document using the default printer settings:

1.   Press Shift+F7 or open the File menu and select
     Print/Fax. The Print dialog box appears.

2.   Select 1. Full Document.

3.   Press Enter to select the Print button. WordPerfect
     prints one copy of your document.

> **Printer Problems.** If your printer does not start
> printing, make sure your printer is on, has paper,
> and is on-line (most printers have a light that
> shows when the printer is on-line). Then, skip to
> the end of this lesson, and display the Control Printer
> screen. This screen often provides the information you
> need to correct the problem.

Setting the Print Options

When you press Shift+F7 or select **P**rint/Fax from the **F**ile
menu, the Print dialog box appears, offering several options

that allow you to tell WordPerfect how to print the document. Table 7.1 provides a brief overview of the available options. To select an option, type the number or highlighted letter in the option's name, or click on the option with your mouse. Select the Print button to start printing.

Table 7.1 WordPerfect's Print dialog box options.

Option	Description
Print	
Full Document	Prints all the pages of the currently displayed document
Page	Prints only the current page of the document
Document on Disk	Prints a document file that is on disk but not opened in WordPerfect (you must enter the name and location of the file)
Multiple Pages	Prints one or more pages of a document
Blocked Text	Lets you print a selected block of text (Lesson 8 explains how to select text)
Options	
Control Printer	Lets you stop and continue printing, as explained in the following section
Print Preview	Lets you view the document, as explained earlier
Initialize Printer	Tells WordPerfect to download soft fonts to your printer
Fax Services	Allows you to print the document to a fax board (assuming your computer has a fax board)

continues

Table 7.1 Continued.

Option	Description
Print Job Graphically	Tells WordPerfect to print text as graphics
Number of Copies	Allows you to print more than one copy of a document
Generated By	Allows you to specify whether you want WordPerfect, your printer, or your network to generate the multiple copies
Output Options	Allows you to enter specific settings for your printer, such as which paper bin you want to use
Document Settings	
Text Quality	Controls the quality of the printed text (higher quality looks better but takes longer to print)
Graphics Quality	Controls the quality of any graphic elements you add to your document, such as clip art or lines
Print Color	Allows you to print in black-and-white or color (if you have a color printer)

The soft fonts referred to under the Initialize Printer option are typestyles and sizes that some printers, usually laser printers, can use. If you have a printer that uses soft fonts, the best time to initialize the printer is before you create the document.

Stopping and Continuing the Print Operation

If you start printing a document and then decide to stop printing for whatever reason, you can stop printing and even cancel the print job, as follows:

1. Press Shift+F7 or open the File menu and select Print/Fax.

2. Select 6. Control Printer. The Control Printer dialog box appears, as shown in Figure 7.3.

3. Use the arrow keys or mouse to highlight the print job you want to cancel and press the space bar. (To select all print jobs, choose 4. (Un)mark All.) An asterisk appears to the left of each selected print job.

4. To stop printing, select Stop. (When you stop a print job, you can resume it later.) To cancel a print job, select 1. Cancel Job. (If you cancel a job you cannot resume it later; you have to start over.)

5. If you stop a job and decide to continue it, select Go to continue.

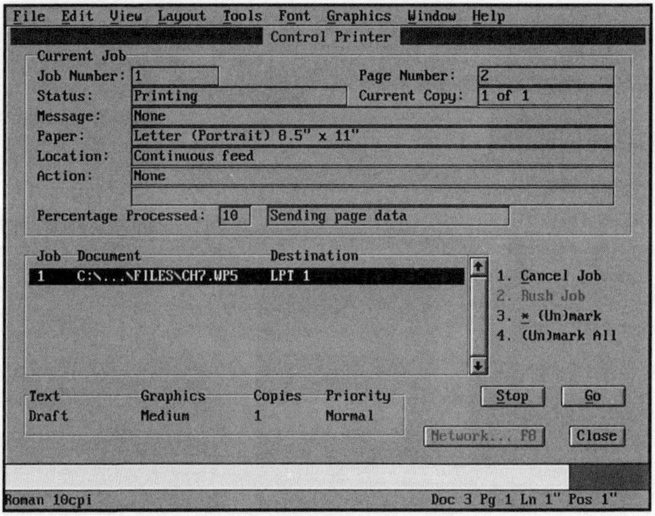

Figure 7.3 The Control Printer dialog box lets you stop, cancel, and continue print jobs.

In this lesson, you learned how to preview your document before printing it, how to print a document, and how to control the print operation. In the next lesson, you will learn how to edit your document by working with blocks of text.

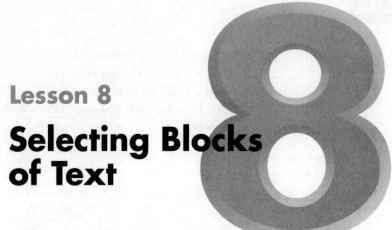

Lesson 8
Selecting Blocks of Text

In this lesson, you learn how to select blocks of text using the mouse or the keyboard.

Understanding Text Blocks

A text block consists of any text that you mark or highlight. When you mark a section of text (a character, word, sentence, or other selection), you form a text block, as shown in Figure 8.1. You can then perform some operation on the selected text, such as deleting or copying the text, changing the margins for the text block, or even making the text bold or italic.

In this lesson, you learn how to select text blocks using the mouse or keyboard. In later lessons, you learn how to perform operations on selected text blocks.

Selecting a Block with the Keyboard

To select a text block with your keyboard, perform the following steps:

1. Move the cursor to the beginning or end of the block you want to mark. This position is your pivot point, allowing you to stretch the highlight over the text.

2. Press Alt+F4 or open the Edit menu and select Block. Blockon appears in the lower left corner of the screen.

3. Use the arrow keys to move the cursor to the opposite end of the block you want to mark. The text is now marked, and you can perform a block operation on the text; for example, you can press F6 to make the text bold.

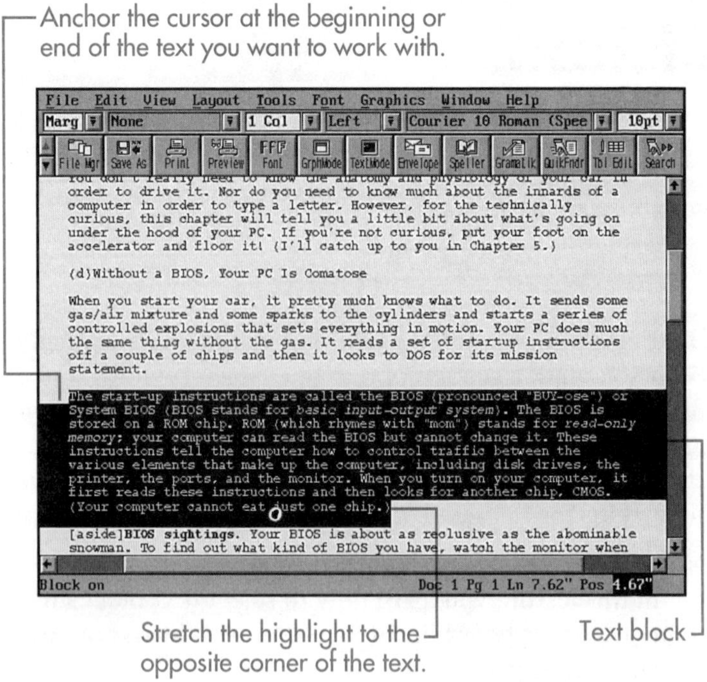

Anchor the cursor at the beginning or end of the text you want to work with.

Stretch the highlight to the opposite corner of the text.

Text block

Figure 8.1 To work with text, you must first select the block you want to work with.

Fast stretch. Although you can stretch the highlight by using the arrow keys, you can also stretch it forward to a specific character, a punctuation mark, or to the end of a paragraph. Simply type the character or punctuation mark, or press Enter to move to the end of a paragraph.

Selecting a Block with the Mouse

If you have a mouse, you can use the mouse to stretch the highlight over the desired text by following these steps:

1. Move the mouse pointer to the first or last character you want to mark.

2. Hold down the mouse button. This anchors the cursor.

3. Drag the highlight to the opposite end of the block, and release the mouse button. The selected block appears highlighted.

Selecting a Sentence, Paragraph, or Page

Although stretching the highlight over text is the most precise way to select text, you may want to work with more logical units of text: sentences, paragraphs, and pages. For example, if you want to move a sentence from the end of a paragraph to the beginning, you can mark the sentence, cut it, and then paste it. Take these steps to select a sentence, paragraph, or page:

1. Move the cursor anywhere inside the sentence, paragraph, or page you want to select. (You can use the keyboard or mouse.)

2. Open the Edit menu and choose Select. The Select submenu appears, as shown in Figure 8.2.

3. Select Sentence, Paragraph, or Page. The sentence, paragraph, or page appears highlighted.

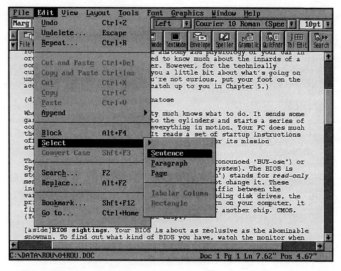

Figure 8.2   The Select submenu allows you to work with more logical units of text.

The last two options on the Select submenu, **T**abular Column and **R**ectangle, allow you to select text in vertical columns, rather than text that is wrapped as in a paragraph.

In this lesson, you learned how to select text blocks. In the next lesson, you learn how to delete, undelete, cut, copy, and paste text blocks in your document.

Lesson 9

Deleting, Copying, and Pasting a Text Block

In this lesson, you learn how to delete, cut, copy, and paste marked blocks of text in a document.

Before you start deleting, cutting, and copying text, you should be familiar with the difference between those three actions:

Delete removes the text block from the document and puts it in the delete buffer, which holds the three most recent deletions. You can press Esc to restore the block.

Cut removes the text block from the document and places it on an unseen clipboard, as shown in Figure 9.1. You can then paste the text block from the clipboard into another document or somewhere else in the same document. (If you cut or copy another text block, the second text block replaces the first on the clipboard, and the first text block is lost.)

Copy leaves the text block in the document and places an exact duplicate on the clipboard. You can then paste the text block into another document or somewhere else in the current document.

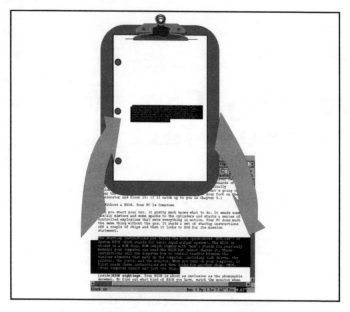

Figure 9.1   When you cut or copy a text block, it is placed on an imaginary clipboard.

Deleting a Text Block

In Lesson 5, you learned how to delete individual characters and words. However, deleting a paragraph or page one character at a time can be time-consuming. To delete a section of text more quickly, take the following steps:

1. Mark the text block, as explained in Lesson 8.

2. Press the Del or Backspace key. The selected block is deleted.

Undoing a Deletion

If you delete a text block by mistake or decide you want it back, you can get the text back in either of two ways: by undoing the deletion or by undeleting the text. Undo is faster, but it can undo only the most recent change to the document. For example, if you delete text and then make some text bold, undo only unbolds the text. Undelete, on the other hand, lets you recover your three most recent deletions. To undo a deletion, perform the following steps:

1. Press Ctrl+Z or open the Edit menu and select Undo.

2. To undo the undo (and redelete the text), press Ctrl+Z or open the Edit menu and select Undo.

> **Undeleting text.** To undelete text, move the cursor where you want the text inserted, press the Esc key, and select 1. Restore. For more information about undeleting text, refer to Lesson 5.

Cutting a Text Block

To cut a text block and place it on the clipboard, take the following steps:

1. Mark the text block you want to cut, as explained in Lesson 8.

2. Press Ctrl+X or open the Edit menu (see Figure 9.2) and select Cut. The marked text is removed from the document and placed on the clipboard. You can now paste the block somewhere else in the document.

> **Quick cut and paste.** A faster way to cut and paste is to mark the block and then press Ctrl+Del or open the Edit menu and select Cut and Paste. The block is removed from the document. Move the cursor where you want the block pasted, and press Enter.

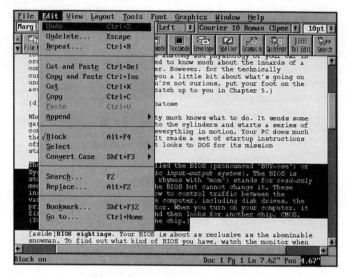

Figure 9.2 The **E**dit menu contains the options for cutting, copying, and pasting blocks.

Copying a Text Block

To copy a text block from your document to the clipboard, perform the following steps:

1. Mark the text block you want to copy, as explained in Lesson 8.

2. Press Ctrl+C or open the Edit menu and select Copy. The marked text remains in the document, and a copy of the block is placed on the clipboard.

> **Quick copy and paste.** A faster way to copy and paste is to mark the block and then press Ctrl+Ins or open the **E**dit menu and select Copy and Paste. Move the cursor where you want the block pasted, and press Enter.

If you want to copy a block to the clipboard without replacing the block that's already on the clipboard, mark the block and then open the Edit menu, select Append, and select To Clipboard. The block is tacked on to the end of the clipboard.

Pasting a Text Block

Once you have cut or copied a block to the clipboard, the block remains on the clipboard until you quit WordPerfect or cut or copy other text to the clipboard. You can paste the clipboard's contents anywhere else in the same document, or in a different document, by taking the following steps:

1. Move the cursor where you want to paste the block. (You can press Shift+F3 to move to a different document window, or you can use the File/Open command to open a document.)

2. Press Ctrl+V or open the Edit menu and select Paste. The block is pasted at the cursor location.

In this lesson, you learned how to delete, cut, copy, and paste text blocks in a document. In the next lesson, you'll learn how to change the appearance of your text.

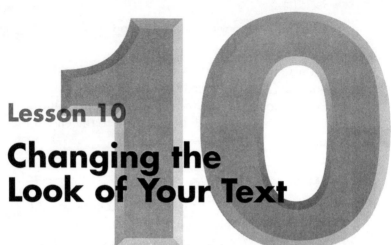

Lesson 10

Changing the Look of Your Text

In this lesson, you learn how to change the appearance of your text by adding attributes, such as bold, italics, and underlining.

What Is an Attribute?

When you start typing a document, whatever you type appears in plain text. If you want to set off a section of the text or emphasize a word or phrase, you can enhance the text by adding an attribute, such as bold, italics, or underlining. With an attribute, the size and design of the type remains the same, but the look, relative size, or position of the text changes. Figure 10.1 shows examples of the available attributes.

Font. A family of text that shares the same design and size is known as a *font*. For example, Courier 10-point is a font. Courier is the design (or typestyle) and 10-point is the size (there are 72 points in an inch). You learn how to change fonts in Lesson 12.

Appearance Attributes

Bold   <u>Underline</u>   <u>Double Underline</u>

Italics   O̶u̶t̶l̶i̶n̶e̶   **Shadow**

S̲mall̲ C̲aps̲   Redline   ~~Strikeout~~

Relative Size

Normal   Fine   Small   Large

Very Large   Extra Large

Position

Normal   Superscript^sup   Subscript_sub

Figure 10.1   WordPerfect's attributes.

Enhancing Text as You Type

You can enhance existing text (as explained later in this lesson), or you can enhance text as you type. To enhance text as you type, turn the enhancement on, type your text, and then turn the enhancement off, as in the following steps:

1. Move the cursor where you want the enhanced text to appear.

2. Open the Font menu, as shown in Figure 10.2, and select the desired attribute; for example, select Bold. If you select Size/Position, a submenu appears.

3. If a submenu appears, select the desired attribute from the submenu.

4. To use multiple attributes (for example, bold italic), repeat steps 2 and 3 for each attribute you want to use.

5. Type the text as you normally would.

6. Open the Font menu and select Normal to turn off the attribute, or press the → key.

> **Quick Bold and Underline.** To turn on Bold or Underline, you can bypass the **Font** menu. To turn on Bold, press F6. To turn on Underline, press F8.

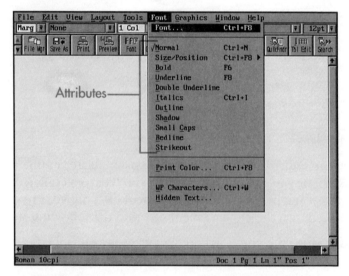

Figure 10.2 Select an attribute from the **Font** menu, and type your text.

Enhancing Existing Text

To enhance existing text, perform the following steps:

1. Mark the text you want to enhance.

2. Open the Font menu and select the desired attribute; for example, select Bold. If you select Size/Position, a submenu appears.

3. If a submenu appears, select the desired attribute from the menu.

4. To use multiple attributes, repeat steps 1 through 3 for each attribute you want to use.

Using the Font Dialog Box to Enhance Text

The easiest way to apply several attributes to a text block is to display the Font dialog box, shown in Figure 10.3, and select each attribute you want to apply. The following steps lead you through the process:

1. Mark the text you want to enhance, or move the cursor where you want to start typing the enhanced text.

2. Press Ctrl+F8, or open the Font menu and select Font. The Font dialog box appears, as in Figure 10.3.

3. Select 3. Appearance, 4. Relative Size, or 5. Position. When you select one of these attribute groups, a number appears next to each attribute in the group.

4. Select the attribute you want to apply. An X appears in the check box next to the attribute, showing that it is on. (You can select the attribute again to turn it off.)

5. Repeat steps 3 and 4 for each attribute you want to turn on.

6. Select the OK button or press Enter.

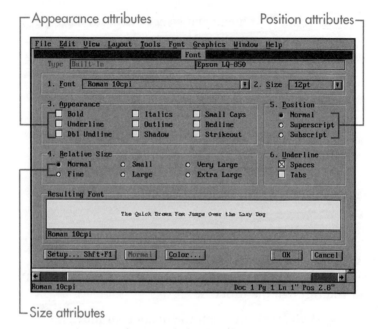

Figure 10.3 The Font dialog box lets you apply all the attributes at the same time.

In this lesson, you learned how to enhance text by applying attributes to the text. Whenever you apply an attribute, WordPerfect inserts codes that turn the attribute on and off. In the next lesson, you will learn how to view and work with these codes.

Lesson 11

Working with WordPerfect Codes

In this lesson, you learn how to view the codes that WordPerfect uses to control your document and how to work with those codes.

What Are WordPerfect Codes?

In the previous lesson, you enhanced text by making the text bold or italic or assigning the text some other attribute. Whenever you enhance text, WordPerfect inserts two codes—one that turns the attribute on and another that turns it off. These codes work in the background to control the appearance of your text. WordPerfect adds the following three types of codes to documents:

- **Paired codes.** Codes used for turning an attribute on and off are called paired codes because WordPerfect always inserts two codes.

- **Open codes.** Open codes (such as codes that control the left and right margins) control the text from the current position of the code up to the next open code that changes the same format setting or to the end of the document.

- **Single codes.** Unlike open codes that control formatting from the current position forward, single codes act only at the current position. For example, when you press the Enter key at the end of a paragraph, WordPerfect inserts a hard return code.

Why worry about codes? Normally, you don't have to think about the codes; they do their work in the background. However, if your text looks funny on-screen or in print, or if your margins are not turning out as expected, you can view the codes to find the cause of the problem and correct it.

Revealing Hidden Codes

You're probably wondering what these codes look like. To view the codes, you can display the Reveal Codes screen shown in Figure 11.1. To turn Reveal Codes on or off, perform any of the following steps:

- Press Alt+F3.

- Press F11.

- Open the View menu and select Reveal Codes.

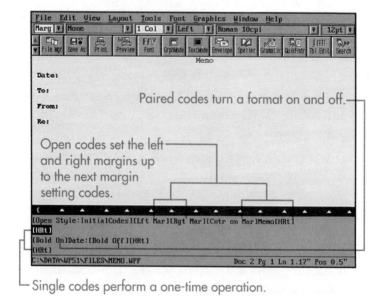

Figure 11.1 The Reveal Codes screen shows you the codes that control your text.

With Reveal Codes on, the screen is split in two; normal text appears in the top part of the screen, and the text with codes appears in the lower part. You can type, edit, and format your document as you normally would, but now you can work with the codes as well.

Editing Codes

Once the codes are displayed, you can edit the codes to change the look and layout of your text. In most cases, editing consists of deleting the code. For example, if you want to unbold some text, you can delete the [Bold On] or [Bold Off] code. To delete a code, perform the following steps:

1. Press Alt+F3 to turn on Reveal Codes.

2. Use the arrow keys to highlight the code or click on it with your mouse. (If you want to delete a paired code, highlight either code in the pair.)

3. Press the Del key. The code is deleted. If you delete one code of a paired code, both codes are deleted.

If you want to change the settings put in place by an open code (for example, you want to change the line spacing), you have two options. The first option is to delete the code and then repeat the steps you used to insert the code in the first place. The problem with this technique is that it does not allow you to adjust the settings. For example, if you delete a code that specified margin settings for a paragraph, when you attempt to enter new margin settings, the old settings are not displayed.

A better way to adjust open code settings is to move the cursor just past the code, change the setting as you normally would, and then delete the old code (the one on the left). When you are ready to change the setting, the old settings are displayed, and you can adjust them rather than entering entirely new settings.

Understanding Automatic Code Placement

Whenever you enter a format setting that inserts an open code in your document, WordPerfect inserts the code at the most logical place in the document. For example, if you change the margins for a paragraph, WordPerfect inserts the code at the beginning of the paragraph, replacing any Left/Right Margin code that might already exist.

If codes are not inserted at logical positions, you or someone else may have inadvertently turned off Auto Code Placement. To determine whether Auto Code Placement is on, perform the following steps:

1. Press Shift+F1 or open the File menu and select Setup.

2. Select Environment.

3. If there is no X in the Auto Code Placement check box, type T or click on Auto Code Placement to turn it on.

In this lesson, you learned how to display WordPerfect's hidden formatting codes, delete codes, and change the settings for open codes. You also learned how to turn Auto Code Placement on or off. In the next lesson, you learn how to work with different type styles and sizes.

Lesson 12

Working with Fonts

In this lesson, you learn how to change the type size and typeface (type design) for an entire document and for selected text.

What Is a Font?

A *font* (pronounced fahnt) is any set of characters that has the same *typeface* and *type size*. For example, Roman 10-point is a font. Roman is the typeface, and 10-point is the size (there are 72 *points* in an inch). The following list shows examples of various fonts:

Roman (12-point)   Times (16-point)

Roman (14-point)   Times (18-point)

Sans Serif (5 cpi)   Helvetica (10-point)

Sans Serif (10 cpi)   Helvetica (12-point)

In WordPerfect, you can change fonts at three levels. First, you can change the *setup initial font* to specify which font you want WordPerfect to use for all new documents. If you start a new document and you don't want to use the setup initial font for the document, you can override the setup initial font by specifying a *document initial font*. You can then override the document initial font within a document by specifying a font for a single letter, word, heading, or other text block.

Changing the Font for All New Documents

When you install WordPerfect, WordPerfect selects a default font based on the installed printer. Unless you specify otherwise, this default font (the setup initial font) is used for all new documents. To change the setup initial font, perform the following steps:

1. Press Ctrl+F8 or open the Font menu and select Font. The Font dialog box appears, as shown in Figure 12.1.

2. Press Shift+F1 or click on the Setup button in the lower left corner of the dialog box. The Font Setup dialog box appears.

3. Choose 1. Select Initial Font. The Initial Font dialog box appears, as shown in Figure 12.2.

4. Select 1. Font, and choose the typestyle you want to use.

5. Select 2. Size, and choose the type size you want to use.

6. Select 4. All New Documents to use the selected font for all new documents you create.

7. Tab to the OK button and press Enter or click on the OK button with your mouse.

Previously created documents. The new setup initial font affects the current document and any new documents. To change the font in a previously created document, you must open the document and change the document initial font as explained in the next section.

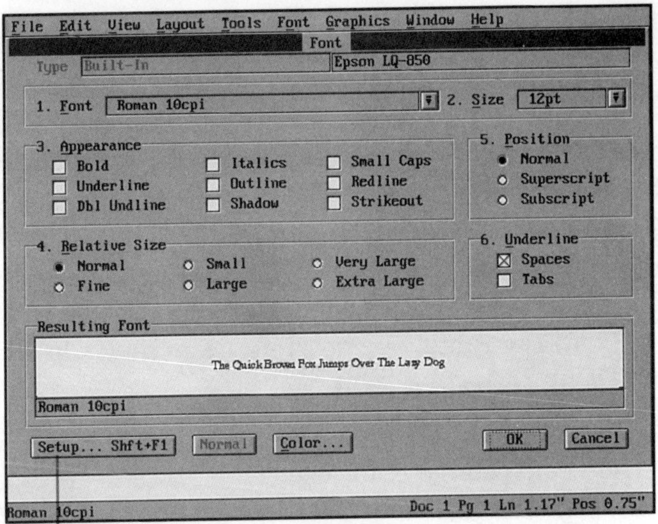

Select the Setup button to choose a
default font for all new documents.

Figure 12.1   The Font dialog box lets you select a font.

Choose the type style you want to use.

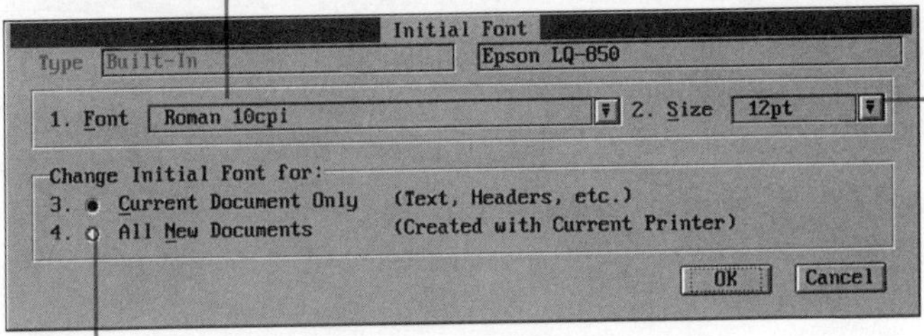

Choose this option to use   Choose a type size.
the selected font for all
new documents.

Figure 12.2   The Initial Font dialog box lets you specify the
font to use for all new documents.

Changing the Font for a Single Document

Now that you have specified a setup initial font, that font is in effect for any new documents you create. If you want to override the setup initial font for a single document, you can choose a document initial font by performing the following steps:

1. Press Ctrl+F8 or open the Font menu and select Font. The Font dialog box appears, as shown in Figure 12.1.

2. Press Shift+F1 or click on the Setup button in the lower left corner of the dialog box. The Font Setup dialog box appears.

3. Choose 1. Select Initial Font. The Initial Font dialog box appears, as shown in Figure 12.2.

4. Select 1. Font, and choose the typestyle you want to use.

5. Select 2. Size, and choose the type size you want to use.

6. Select 3. Current Document Only.

7. Tab to the OK button and press Enter or click on the OK button with your mouse.

Changing the Font within a Document

The characters you type appear in the setup initial font or document initial font. To override either of these default font settings, perform the following steps:

1. Mark the text whose font you want to change (see Lesson 8), or move the cursor where you want to start typing the text.

2. Press Ctrl+F8, or open the Font menu and select Font. The Font dialog box appears, as in Figure 12.1.

3. Select 1. Font. A list of available fonts appears.

4. Use the arrow keys to highlight the desired font and press Enter, or double-click on the font.

5. To change the size of the text, select 2. Size.

6. Use the arrow keys to highlight the desired type size and press Enter, or double-click on the size with your mouse.

7. (Optional) You can assign attributes (such as bold and italics) to the text as explained in Lesson 10.

8. Select the OK button or press Enter.

In this lesson, you learned how to change the default font for all new documents and for a single document. You also learned how to override the default font settings for selected text within a document. In the next lesson, you learn how to change the tab stop settings to align text.

Lesson 13

Setting Tabs

In this lesson, you learn how to tell WordPerfect where to place the cursor when you press the Tab key.

What Are Tabs?

Whenever you press the Tab key in a document, WordPerfect moves the cursor (and any text that's to the right of the cursor) to a *tab stop*. Unless you specify otherwise, tab stops are set at half-inch intervals from the left margin. So, if you press the Tab key once, the cursor moves one-half inch in from the left margin. Press Tab again, and the cursor moves another half-inch interval.

Viewing the Tab Stop Settings

You can view the current tab stop settings at any time by performing the following steps:

1. Move the cursor anywhere inside the paragraph whose tab stop settings you want to view.

2. Press Shift+F8 or open the Layout menu.

3. Select Line. The Line Format dialog box appears.

4. Select 1. Tab Set. The Tab Set dialog box appears, as shown in Figure 13.1.

5. To close the Tab Set dialog box, click on the OK button or Cancel button, or tab to either button and press Enter.

6. To close the Line Format dialog box, press Enter.

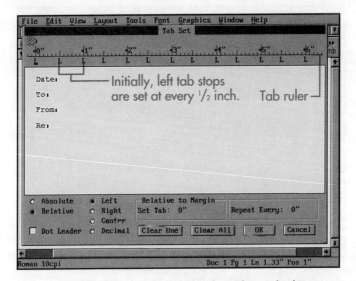

Figure 13.1 The Tab Set dialog box shows the location and type of each tab stop.

> **Tab stop ruler.** The tab stop ruler at the top of the Tab Set dialog box shows the location and type of each tab stop. The settings on the ruler control the text from the cursor position to the end of the document or up to the point at which you change the tab stop settings again.

Types of Tab Stops

Initially, all tab stops are left tab stops; that is, any text you type at the tab stop is aligned flush left against the stop. You can change the type of tab stop to center the text, right-align it, or align a decimal point on the tab stop (for aligning a column of numbers). Figure 13.2 shows the various types of tab stops and how you might use them.

The type of tab stop is identified by the first letter in its name.

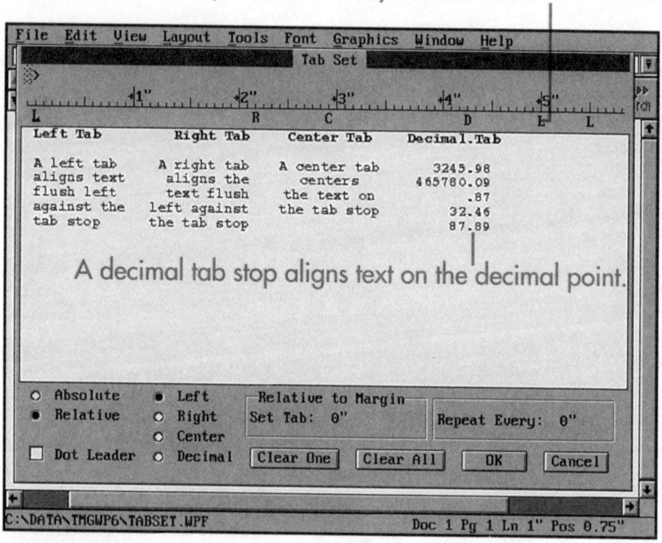

A decimal tab stop aligns text on the decimal point.

Figure 13.2 Text aligns differently depending on the type of tab stop.

Clearing Tab Stops

As you see in Figure 13.1, the tab stop ruler can get very cluttered with the various tab stop settings. If you need to use only two or three tab stop settings, you may want to clear some. That way, you don't have to press the Tab key several times to move to the desired tab stop. To clear tab stop settings, perform the following steps:

1. Move the cursor anywhere inside the paragraph whose tab stop settings you want to clear, or start a new paragraph.
2. Open the Layout menu, select Line, and select 1. Tab Set to display the Tab Set dialog box.
3. To clear only one tab stop setting, use the arrow keys to move to the setting, or click on it with your mouse.

4. To clear only one setting, press the Del key or select Clear One; to clear all the settings, select Clear All.

5. To close the Tab Set dialog box, click on the OK button or Cancel button, or tab to either button and press Enter.

6. To close the Line Format dialog box, press Enter.

> **Canceling your changes.** You can cancel your tab stop setting changes by clicking on the Cancel button or tabbing to it and pressing Enter.

Adding Tab Stops

You can add tab stop settings to the tab ruler at any point in the document by performing the following steps:

1. Move the cursor anywhere inside the paragraph whose tab stops you want to set, or start a new paragraph.

2. Open the Layout menu, select Line, and select 1. Tab Set to display the Tab Set dialog box.

3. (Optional) Clear any tabs as described in the previous section.

4. Use the arrow keys to move the cursor to the place on the tab ruler where you want to set a tab stop. (You can type over an existing tab stop setting to change the type of tab at that position.)

5. Type the first letter of the type of tab stop you want to set: L for Left, R for Right, C for Center, or D for Decimal.

6. Repeat steps 4 and 5 for any additional tab stops you want to set.

Moving a tab stop. Instead of deleting and then setting a tab stop, you can move an existing tab stop. Use the arrow keys to move the cursor under the tab stop you want to move. Hold down the Ctrl key and use the left or right arrow key to move the tab stop where you want it.

Working with the Tab Set Code

Whenever you change the tab stop settings, WordPerfect inserts a [Tab Set] code at the beginning of the paragraph. This code tells WordPerfect where the tab stops are set. To return the tab stops to the original settings, press Alt+F3 to display the Reveal Codes screen, highlight the [Tab Set] code, and press Del. (When you highlight the [Tab Set] code in Reveal Codes, the code expands to show the tab stop settings.)

If you change the tab stop settings for a paragraph, WordPerfect automatically replaces the existing [Tab Set] code with a new [Tab Set] code that contains the current settings.

In this lesson, you learned how to align text by changing tab stop settings. In the next lesson, you learn how to change the line spacing and change the alignment of text in other ways.

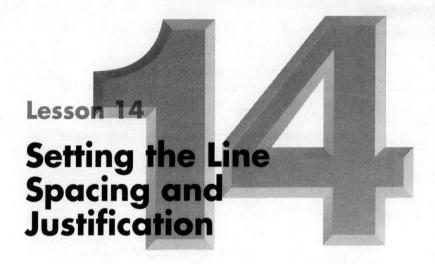

Lesson 14

Setting the Line Spacing and Justification

In this lesson, you learn how to change the line spacing for an entire document or a portion of it and how to align text between the left and right margins.

Changing the Line Spacing

As you type, WordPerfect single-spaces the text, so no extra space is inserted between each line of text. Sometimes, however, you may want to double-space or triple-space your text. For example, you may wish to leave extra space between lines to write comments.

You can change the line spacing for an entire document or a section of it by performing the following steps:

1. Press Home,Home,↑ to move the cursor to the top of the document, or move the cursor anywhere in the document where you want the line spacing to change.

2. Press Shift+F8 or open the Layout menu.

3. Select Line. The Line Format dialog box appears, as shown in Figure 14.1.

4. Select 3. Line Spacing. The cursor moves to the Line Spacing text box.

5. Type the desired line spacing setting. (You can type a decimal entry, for example, **2.5**, to add 2.5 line spaces between each line.)

Or, click on the up or down arrow to the right of the Line Spacing text box (or press Alt+↑ or Alt+↓) to increase or decrease the setting in increments of .10 (one-tenth of an inch).

6. Press F7 or click on the OK button to accept the setting. If you pressed Shift+F8 to display the Format dialog box, you return to that dialog box. Press Enter to close it.

Enter the line spacing Setting here.

```
┌──────────────────────── Line Format ────────────────────────┐
│                                                              │
│  1. Tab Set...  Rel: -1",-0.5",+0",+0.5",+1",+1.5",+2",...   │
│                                                              │
│  ┌─2. Justification───────────┐  ┌─Hyphenation───────────┐   │
│  │    ● Left                  │  │  6. ☐ Hyphenation     │   │
│  │    ○ Center                │  └───────────────────────┘   │
│  │    ○ Right                 │  7. Hyphenation Zone          │
│  │    ○ Full                  │        Left:  [10] %          │
│  │    ○ Full, All Lines       │        Right: [4]  %          │
│  └────────────────────────────┘                              │
│                                                              │
│  3. Line Spacing: [1.0]  [▲▼]  ┌─8. Line Height──────────┐    │
│                                │    ● Auto                │    │
│  4. Line Numbering... [Off]    │    ○ Fixed:              │    │
│                                └─────────────────────────┘    │
│  5. Paragraph Borders...                                     │
│                                      [  OK  ]  [Cancel]       │
│                                                              │
└──────────────────────────────────────────────────────────────┘
```

These buttons allow you to increase or decrease the setting in increments of .10 inch.

Figure 14.1   The Line Format dialog box lets you enter a line spacing setting.

> **Returning to the original line spacing.** To return to the original line spacing setting, press Alt+F3 to turn on Reveal Codes. Highlight the [Ln Spacing] code you just inserted, and press Del. If you want to change the line spacing later in the document, simply move to where you want the line spacing to change, and repeat steps 1 through 6.

To change the line spacing for a single paragraph or any selected text block, first select the text block. Then, perform steps 2 through 6 as just explained. WordPerfect inserts a [+Ln Spacing] code at the beginning of the block and a [-Ln Spacing] code at the end of the block that returns line spacing to its original setting.

Aligning Text: Left, Right, Full, or Center

As you type text, WordPerfect aligns the text against the left margin, leaving the lines uneven at the right. You can change the alignment to center the text, align it against the right margin, or fully justify the text so each line is flush against both the left and right margins (see Figure 14.2). You can change the alignment of text at any point in a document—for a single line, or for a text block. The following sections explain how.

Justification. WordPerfect refers to the various text alignment options as justifications.

Changing Justification in a Document

You can insert a [Just] code anywhere in a document to change the justification from the [Just] code to the end of the document or up to the next [Just] code. To change the justification, perform the following steps:

1. Move the cursor anywhere inside the paragraph whose justification you want to change.

2. Press Shift+F8 or open the Layout menu.

3. Select Line. The Line Format dialog box appears.

4. Select 2. Justification.

5. Select the desired justification option.

6. Select the OK button. If you pressed Shift+F8 to display the Format dialog box, you return to that dialog box. Press Enter to close it. The current paragraph and any paragraphs that follow it are realigned according to the specified justification.

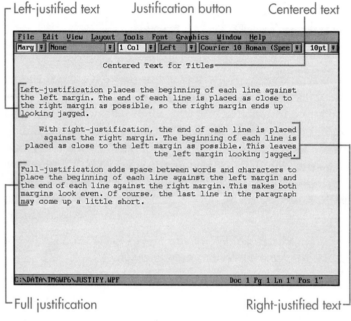

Left-justified text   Justification button   Centered text

Full justification   Right-justified text

Figure 14.2 WordPerfect can justify text in various ways.

> **Quick justification with the ribbon.** If you turned on the ribbon (**V**iew/**R**ibbon), you can use the justification drop-down menu to change the justification quickly. Move the mouse pointer over the justification button (see Figure 14.2), hold down the mouse button, and drag the highlight over the desired justification option. When you release the mouse button, WordPerfect realigns the text according to the selected justification.

Centering or Right-Justifying a Single Line

To center a single line, move the cursor in the line and press Shift+F6. To right-justify a single line (for example, a date at the top of a letter), move the cursor in the line and press Alt+F6.

Changing the Justification for a Text Block. To change the alignment for a text block, select the text (refer to Lesson 8). Open the Layout menu, select Justification, and select the desired justification option.

Indenting Text

Sometimes, you may need to indent text to create a list or to set the text apart from surrounding text. For example, you may want to place a long quote in a separate paragraph. WordPerfect provides you with three options for indenting text: left indent, left/right indent, and hanging indent (see Figure 14.3).

To indent a paragraph, perform the following steps:

1. Move the cursor to the first character of the paragraph you want to indent.

2. Open the Layout menu and select Alignment. The Alignment submenu opens.

3. Select the desired indent option: Indent →, Indent →←← or Hanging Indent. WordPerfect inserts a [Indent] code and indents the text as specified. (The **B**ack Tab option moves the cursor back one tab stop; this is useful for creating a hanging indent.)

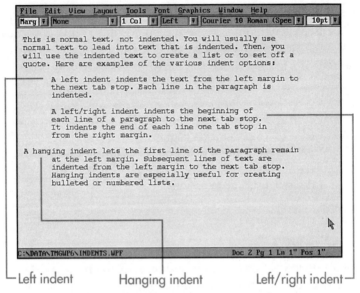

Figure 14.3 You can use indents to create lists or to set text apart from surrounding text.

If you decide later that you do not want the text to be indented, delete the [Indent] code. A quick way to delete the [Indent] code is to move the cursor to the first character in the paragraph and press the Backspace key.

> **Quick left and left/right indents.** To create a left indent, move the cursor to the beginning of the paragraph and press the F4 key. To create a left/right indent, move the cursor to the beginning of the paragraph and press Shift+F4.

In this lesson, you learned how to change the line spacing and text justification and how to indent text. In the next lesson, you learn how to enter paper size and margin settings for your document.

Lesson 15

Setting the Paper Size and Margins

In this lesson, you learn how to specify the size of the paper you want to print on and how to change the margins for an entire document or a portion of it.

Selecting the Paper Size and Type

Unless you choose otherwise, WordPerfect assumes you want to print on standard 8-1/2-by-11-inch paper in portrait orientation. If you want to print on a different size of paper or in landscape orientation (sideways on a page), you must select a different paper size and/or type.

> **Paper terminology.** You will encounter several new terms when selecting a paper size and type. The *paper size* refers to the actual dimensions of the page (for example, 8-1/2-by-11-inch). *Paper type* specifies the makeup of the paper (for example, letterhead, envelope, or transparency). *Location* specifies how the paper is loaded into the printer (for example, continuous feed paper or manual feed). *Orientation* refers to how the text is printed on the page: *portrait* prints the text straight across the page; *landscape* prints the text sideways, making a page wider than it is long.

You can select a paper size and type from a list of
common paper sizes and types by performing the following
steps.

1. Press Shift+F8 or open the Layout menu.

2. Select Page. The Page Format dialog box appears.

3. Select 4. Paper Size/Type. The Paper Size/Type
    dialog box appears, as shown in Figure 15.1.

4. In the Paper Name list, use the arrow keys to
    highlight the name of the paper on which you want
    to print. The Paper Details show the settings for the
    highlighted paper name.

5. Choose 1. Select. You are returned to the Page
    Format dialog box where the selected paper size
    and type is displayed.

6. Press Enter, or click on the OK button with your
    mouse.

7. If the Format dialog box is displayed, press Enter to
    close it.

Setting the Page Margins

Unless you choose otherwise, WordPerfect uses a 1-inch
margin, setting text 1 inch from the left, right, top, and
bottom edge of the page. You can change any of these
margins for a document by performing the following steps:

1. Press Home,Home,↑ to move the cursor to the top
    of the document. The [Margin] codes affect all text
    from the beginning of the document to the end, or
    up to the next [Margin] code.

2. Press Shift+F8 or open the Layout menu.

3. Select Margins. The Margin Format dialog box appears, as shown in Figure 15.2.

4. To change the left, right, top, or bottom margin, select the margin you want to change, type the new setting (in inches), and press Enter.

5. To indent paragraphs from the left or right margin, choose Left or Right Margin Adjustment, and enter the distance (in inches) that you want to indent the paragraph from the margin.

6. To indent the first line of a paragraph, choose First Line Indent and enter the distance you want the first line of each paragraph indented. (By choosing to indent paragraphs, you won't have to press the Tab key at the beginning of each paragraph.)

7. To insert additional space between paragraphs, choose Paragraph Spacing and type the number of blank lines you want inserted between each paragraph.

Or, click on the up or down arrow to the right of the Paragraph Spacing text box (or press Alt+↑ or Alt+↓) to increase or decrease the setting in increments of .10 (one-tenth of a line).

8. Press Enter or click on the OK button.

9. If the Format dialog box is displayed, press Enter to close it.

The Paper Name list contains several
common paper size/type settings.

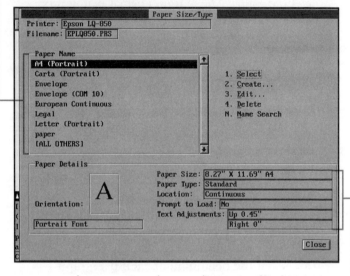

The Paper Details area shows you the dimensions
and orientation of the highlighted paper type.

Figure 15.1   The Paper Size/Type dialog box lets you
choose from a list of common paper sizes and types.

**Setting the Left and Right Margins for
Selected Text.** To change the left and right
margins for selected text, first block the text
(Alt+F4 or by using the mouse), and then perform
steps 2-9 in the previous set of steps.

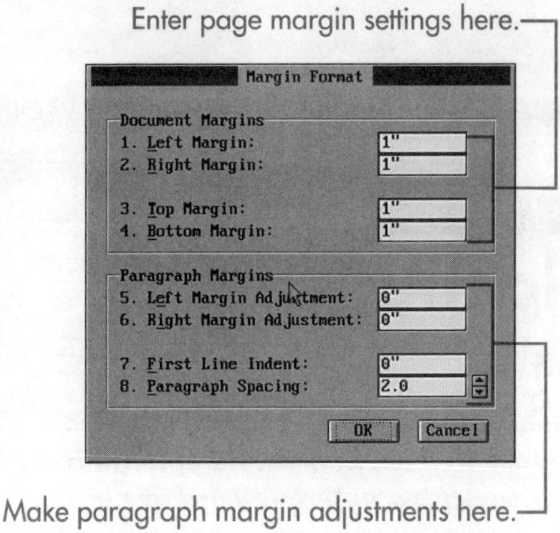

Enter page margin settings here.─┐

Make paragraph margin adjustments here.─┘

Figure 15.2 The Margin Format dialog box.

In this lesson, you learned how to specify the size and type of paper on which you intend to print and how to change the left, right, top, and bottom margins for a document or for paragraphs. In the next lesson, you learn how to search for and replace words, phrases, and other text.

Lesson 16

Searching and Replacing Text

In this lesson, you learn how to have WordPerfect find a word or phrase in a document and optionally replace the word or phrase with a different word or phrase.

Why Search and Replace Text?

Say you write an essay or an article, and you notice that you have overused the word "stuff." You want to use some other words (such as "things" or "items") in place of the word "stuff" in various places. You can use the Search feature to find each occurrence of the desired term, and then you can type a new term in its place.

You can also use the Search and Replace feature to replace each occurrence of the word "stuff" with a different word (such as "belongings" or "supplies"). WordPerfect searches the document for each occurrence of a term and then replaces it with the specified term in a matter of seconds.

Searching for a Text String

WordPerfect can find any text or formatting code in a document. To search for text, perform the following steps:

1. Move the cursor where you want the search to start. You can search forward or backward from this position. (To start from the beginning of the document, press Home,Home,↑.)

2. Press F2 or open the Edit menu and select Search. The Search dialog box appears, as shown in Figure 16.1.

3. Type the text you want WordPerfect to search for.

4. If desired, choose one or more of the following options to tell WordPerfect how to perform the search:

    2.   **Backward Search.** Select this option to tell WordPerfect to search from the cursor position back to the beginning of the document.

    3.   **Case Sensitive Search.** When this option is on, WordPerfect distinguishes between uppercase and lowercase characters. If you search for Johnson, WordPerfect does not find johnson.

    4.   **Find Whole Words Only.** This option tells WordPerfect to skip over occurrences of a text string that are part of another word. For example, if you turn this option on and search for the word "worm," WordPerfect skips over "bookworm."

    5.   **Extended Search.** Extended search tells WordPerfect to search headers, footers, and other text that is not part of the main document for the search string you enter.

5. Press F2 to start the search. WordPerfect hunts down the first occurrence of the specified word or phrase and moves the cursor just past it.

6. To search for the next occurrence of the word or phrase, press F2 twice.

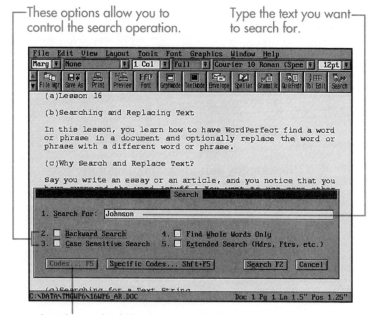

┌─These options allow you to
  control the search operation.

Type the text you want─┐
to search for.

Select the Codes button to insert a
formatting code in the Search For text box.

Figure 16.1   Use the Search dialog box to specify the text you want to find.

Searching for Formatting Codes

In the previous steps, you entered a text string to have WordPerfect search for a specific word or phrase. It is often useful to search for codes as well. For example, if you want to find all the bolded text in a document, you can have WordPerfect search for the [Bold On] code.

> **Turn on Reveal Codes.** When searching for formatting codes, it's a good idea to have the codes displayed. Press Alt+F3 or open the View menu and select Reveal Codes.

To search for a code, perform the following steps:

1. Move the cursor where you want the search to start.

2. Press F2 or open the Edit menu and select Search.

3. Press F5, or click on the Codes button to display a list of codes, as shown in Figure 16.2. (The Specific Codes Shift+F5 button lets you search for the following codes: Advance, Overstrike, Font Change, Line Spacing, Justification, and Margins.)

4. Highlight the code you want to search for, and press Enter or click on the Select button. You return to the Search dialog box, and the selected code is placed in the Search For text box.

5. (Optional) You can enter additional codes and/or text in the text box.

6. Press F2 to start the search. WordPerfect hunts down the first occurrence of the specified code and moves the cursor just past it.

7. To search for the next occurrence of the code, press F2 twice.

Don't type the code. Although it looks as
though you can type a code in the Search For text
box, if you type the code, WordPerfect searches
for text, not for a formatting code. You must press
F5 or Shift+F5 and select the code from the code list.

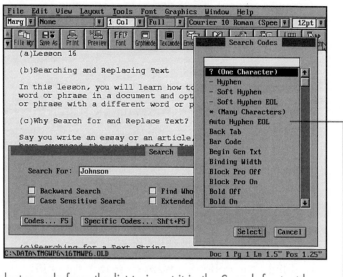

Select a code from the list to insert it in the Search for text box.

Figure 16.2   Select the code you want to search for from the
list of codes.

Replacing a Text String

The Search and Replace feature allows you to replace one
word, phrase, or code with another word, phrase, or code.
To replace text and/or codes, perform the following steps:

1.   Move the cursor where you want the search and
     replace operation to start. WordPerfect searches
     and replaces from the cursor position forward or
     back.

2. Press Alt+F2 or open the Edit menu and select Replace. The Search and Replace dialog box appears, as shown in Figure 16.3.

3. In the Search For text box, type the text you want to replace. (You can replace codes by pressing F5 and selecting the code.)

4. Press Enter. The cursor moves into the Replace With text box.

5. Type the text you want to insert in place of the Search For text. (Again, you can insert codes by pressing F5 and selecting the desired code.)

6. Select 3. Confirm Replacement if you want WordPerfect to ask for your okay before replacing a word or phrase.

7. Select any of the other replacement options, as desired, to control the search and replace operation.

8. Press F2 or select the Replace button. WordPerfect performs the replace operation as specified.

9. If you turn Confirm Replacement on, WordPerfect displays a message asking if you are sure you want to replace this occurrence of the word or phrase. Select Yes to replace the term, No to skip it, or Replace All to replace all occurrences without asking for your okay.

You can combine
text and codes in the
Search For text box.

Enter replacement
text and/or codes here.

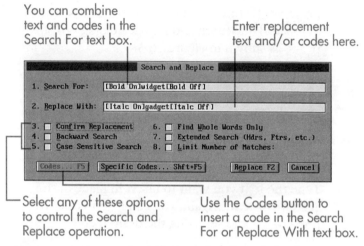

Select any of these options
to control the Search and
Replace operation.

Use the Codes button to
insert a code in the Search
For or Replace With text box.

Figure 16.3 Use the Search and Replace dialog box to
specify your search and replace preferences.

In this lesson, you learned how to have WordPerfect
search for and optionally replace specific text and codes. In
the next lesson, you learn how to use WordPerfect's writing
tools to further polish your documents.

Lesson 17

Using WordPerfect's Writing Tools

In this lesson, you learn how to use WordPerfect's writing tools: the spell checker, grammar checker, and thesaurus.

Checking Your Spelling

WordPerfect is equipped with a program that can check your document for spelling errors and provide a list of possible corrections. You can check the spelling of a single word or page, of the entire document, or from the cursor position to the end of the document. To run the spell checker, perform the following steps:

1. To check the spelling of a single word or page, or to check it from where the cursor is located to the end of the document, move the cursor where you want the spell checker to start. (If you want to check the entire document, the cursor can be anywhere.)

2. Press Alt+F1 or open the Tools menu and select Writing Tools.

3. Select Speller. The Speller dialog box appears.

4. Select one of the following options to start the spell checker:

    1. **W**ord checks the spelling of the word where the cursor is currently positioned.

    2. **P**age checks the spelling of the current page.

3. **D**ocument checks the spelling of the entire document.

4. **F**rom Cursor checks the spelling from the cursor position to the end of the document.

WordPerfect starts to check for spelling errors. If WordPerfect finds a word that does not match a word in its dictionary, WordPerfect displays the Word Not Found dialog box, as shown in Figure 17.1.

5. If WordPerfect finds a questionable word, take one of the following actions:

Highlight the correct spelling in the Suggestions list and choose 7. Replace Word.

To ignore the word and move on, select 1. Skip Once (to ignore only this occurrence of the word) or 2. Skip in this Document (to ignore every occurrence of this word).

To add the word to WordPerfect's dictionary (so WordPerfect will never question it again), select 3. Add to Dictionary.

To edit the word, choose 4. Edit Word, type your correction, and press Enter.

6. Repeat step 4 until WordPerfect displays a dialog box showing that the spell check is complete.

7. Press Enter to select OK.

Proofread your document. WordPerfect questions only those words that do not match a word in the spell checker's dictionary. If you type "to" when you mean to type "too," WordPerfect skips over the error.

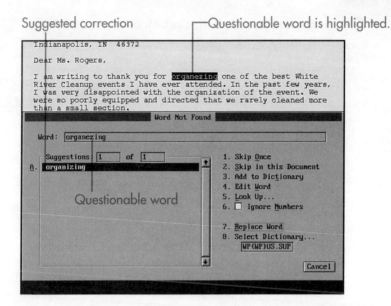

Figure 17.1 The Word Not Found dialog box.

Checking Your Grammar

WordPerfect contains a built-in grammar checker (Grammatik) that can check your document for grammatical problems, such as overuse of the passive voice, misplaced commas, and subject-verb disagreement. To check your document, perform the following steps:

1. Press Alt+F1 or open the Tools menu and select Writing Tools.

2. Select Grammatik. WordPerfect kicks you out to the grammar checking program.

3. Select Interactive check. Grammatik starts to check the grammar of the current document and stops on the first problem it finds, as shown in Figure 17.2.

4. If Grammatik stops on a problem, do one of the following:

   Press F9 and type your correction to the problem.

   Press F10 to skip this problem and go on to the next one.

   Press F6 to ignore the grammar rule that Grammatik is using to discover this particular error. For example, if you love the passive voice, you can choose to have Grammatik ignore your uses of the passive voice.

5. To Quit Grammatik any time during the grammar check, press Alt+Q to open the **Q**uit menu, and then select one of the following options:

   Quit, **S**ave work so far: quits Grammatik and saves your changes to the file.

   Quit, place **B**ookmark: quits Grammatik and inserts a code that allows you to resume the grammar check later from the current position.

   Quit, mark rest of document: quits Grammatik, but inserts comments in the document, showing questionable grammatical constructions.

   Cancel, ignore work so far: quits Grammatik and cancels any changes you made to your document.

6. When Grammatik is finished checking your document, or you choose to quit, you are returned to the Grammatik opening screen. Select Quit to return to WordPerfect.

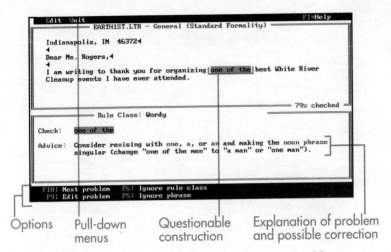

Options   Pull-down   Questionable   Explanation of problem
           menus   construction   and possible correction

Figure 17.2 Grammatik highlights the questionable construction and explains the problem.

> **More about Grammatik.** Grammatik is a
> powerful and complex grammar checking
> program that this book cannot cover in detail. To
> learn more about Grammatik, press F1 when the
> opening screen is displayed to view a list of help topics.
> Highlight the desired topic and press Enter.

Choosing the Best Word with the Thesaurus

WordPerfect is equipped with a thesaurus that can help you find a synonym (a word that has a similar meaning) for one of the words in your document. To view a list of synonyms for a word, perform the following steps:

1. Move the cursor anywhere inside the word whose synonyms you want to see.

2. Press Alt+F1 or open the Tools menu and select Writing Tools.

3. Select **Thesaurus**. The Thesaurus dialog box appears, as shown in Figure 17.3.

4. To replace the highlighted word with one of the words in the list, highlight the desired word in the list and select Replace.

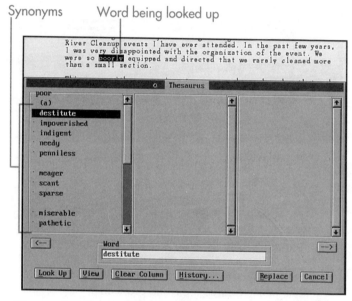

Figure 17.3 The Thesaurus provides a list of synonyms for the selected word.

Expanding the List of Synonyms

Notice that the thesaurus is divided into three columns and that some of the words in the first column are preceded by a dot. If you select a word that is preceded by a dot, a list of synonyms for that word appears in the next column. To view a list of synonyms for a word in the list, perform the following steps:

1. Highlight the word whose synonyms you want to view (it must be preceded by a dot).

2. Press Enter.

3. Repeat steps 1 and 2 in the new column to view another list of synonyms.

> **Shifting columns.** If you choose to view more than two additional columns, the original column remains on-screen, but the other columns start to move off the screen to the left. To bring those columns into view, press the left arrow key or click on the left arrow at the bottom of the Thesaurus until the desired column is displayed. You can then use the right arrow key or the right arrow button to view columns that scroll off the right side of the screen. To clear one of the columns, move the cursor into the column and select **C**lear Column.

Looking Up a Word

In addition to viewing synonyms for a word that's already in the document, you can type a word and have WordPerfect find synonyms for that word. To look up a word, perform the following steps:

1. Choose Look Up. The cursor moves to the Word text box.

2. Type the word you want to look up and press Enter. A list of synonyms appears.

> **Viewing a list of words you have looked up.** The **H**istory button displays a list of all the words you have looked up. To move to the column of synonyms for a word quickly, choose History and then select the word from the list.

In this lesson, you learned how to use WordPerfect's writing tools to help you polish your documents. In the next lesson, you learn how to create tables inside a document.

Lesson 18
Working with Tables

In this lesson, you learn how to create and format tables to organize information in columns.

What Is a Table?

In most word-processing programs, including WordPerfect, you can create columns of text by using tabs. However, if you have text that wraps in a column, getting all the columns to align can be a chore. An easier way to create a table is to use WordPerfect's Table feature. In a table, WordPerfect wraps the text in a column and keeps the text aligned across a row, as shown in Figure 18.1. Tables also allow you to add lines and shading in order to make the table more attractive and useful.

Table terminology. As Figure 18.1 shows, a table consists of a series of *rows* and *columns* that intersect to form boxes called *cells*. You type text in the cells to form your table.

Creating a Table

Creating a basic table is easy; you tell WordPerfect the number of rows and columns you want, and WordPerfect does the rest. To create a basic table, perform the following steps:

1. Press Enter to start a new paragraph for your table.

2. Press Alt+F7 and select Tables, or open the Layout menu and select Tables. The Tables submenu appears.

3. Select Create. The Create Table dialog box appears, as shown in Figure 18.2.

4. Type the number of columns you want in the table, or click on the up or down arrow to the right of the Columns text box to set the number.

5. Tab to the Rows text box, and type the number of rows you want in the table or click on the up or down arrow to the right of the text box. Press Enter.

6. Press Enter or click on the OK button to create the table. WordPerfect creates the table and displays it in the Table Edit screen (more about that later).

7. Press Esc to return to your document. WordPerfect inserts the table at the cursor position.

Row   Column   Cell

Table 18.1[em]Table movement keys.	
To Go	Press
Up one cell	[ua]
Down one cell	[da]
Right one cell	Alt+[ra] or Tab
Left one cell	Alt+[la] or Shift+Tab
First cell in column	Alt+Home,[ua]
Last cell in column	Alt+Home,[da]
First cell in row	Alt+Home,[la]
Last cell in row	Alt+Home,[ra]
Cell in upper left corner	Alt+Home,Home,[ua]
Cell in lower right corner	Alt+Home,Home,[da]

Figure 18.1   A typical WordPerfect table.

Figure 18.2   Specify the desired number of rows and columns.

Moving Around and Typing Text in a Table

To move around in a table, use the mouse to click inside a cell, or use the cursor-movement keys, as shown in Table 18.1. Once in a cell, you can type and format text just as you would normally type and format text. As you type text in a cell, the cell wraps the text and expands as needed.

Table 18.1   Table movement keys.

To Go	Press
Up one cell	↑
Down one cell	↓
Right one cell	Alt+→ or Tab
Left one cell	Alt+← or Shift+Tab
First cell in column	Alt+Home,↑
Last cell in column	Alt+Home,↓
First cell in row	Alt+Home,←
Last cell in row	Alt+Home,→
Cell in upper left corner	Alt+Home,Home,↑
Cell in lower right corner	Alt+Home,Home,↓

Changing the Table's Size and Appearance

Although you can leave the table as it is, you may want to tinker with it by adjusting the width of the columns or the height of the rows, by adding rows or columns, by removing lines or adding shading, or by applying other formats to the table. You can do all this and more by displaying the Table Edit screen, as follows:

1.   Move the cursor anywhere inside the table.

2. Press Alt+F7 and select Tables or open the Layout menu and select Tables.

3. Select Edit. The table appears in the Table Edit screen, as shown in Figure 18.3.

4. Edit the table, as explained in the following sections.

5. Press F7 or click on the Close button.

Row numbers ———————————————————— Columns

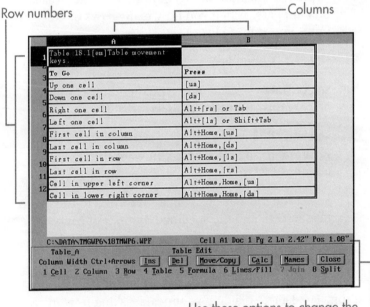

Use these options to change the structure and look of the table.

Figure 18.3 The Table Edit screen lets you modify and format your table.

Quick table edit. If your keyboard has 12 function keys, you can display the Table Edit screen quickly. Move the cursor anywhere inside the table, and press Alt+F11.

Adding or Deleting Rows and Columns

To insert one or more rows or columns into your table, perform the following steps:

1. Display the table in the Table Edit screen.

2. Move the cursor to the row or column where you want the new row or column inserted. (You can insert rows or columns before or after the cursor.)

3. Type **I** or click on the Ins button. The Insert dialog box appears, asking you how many rows or columns you want to insert.

4. Select 1. Columns or 2. Rows.

5. Select 3. How Many? and type the number of rows or columns you want to insert.

6. Select 4. Before Cursor Position or 5. After Cursor Position, to specify where you want the rows or columns inserted.

7. Select the OK button. You are returned to the Table Edit screen, and the specified number of rows or columns are inserted.

To delete rows or columns, move the cursor in the row or column you want to delete, and type **D** or click on the Del button. The Delete dialog box appears, asking how many rows or columns you want to delete. Enter your preferences, and then select the OK button.

Adjusting the Column Width

When you create a table, WordPerfect makes the table as wide as possible and makes the columns all the same width. You can adjust the column width by performing the following steps:

1. Display the table in the Table Edit screen.

2. Move the cursor in any cell in the column whose width you want to adjust.

3. Hold down the Ctrl key while pressing → to make the column wider or ← to make it narrower.

Other Formatting Options

At the bottom of the Table Edit screen are several other formatting options. Although this lesson cannot cover the options in detail, here is a quick list and brief explanation of each option:

1. Cell displays a dialog box that allows you to specify format settings for selected cell(s), including text attributes and text alignment.

2. Column displays the Column Format dialog box which allows you to specify the format settings for selected columns, including text attributes and column margins, and decimal alignment options.

3. Row displays a dialog box that allows you to specify row settings, including row height and margins and whether the text can wrap or not.

4. Table displays the Table Format dialog box that allows you to enter the default format settings for the entire table.

5. Formula allows you to enter a formula in the current cell that uses values from other cells and numerical values to perform a mathematical operation. This is an advanced feature that is beyond the scope of this book.

6. Lines/Fill allows you to specify the type of lines and shading you want to use for selected cells.

7. **J**oin allows you to join two or more cells to create a single cell. To join cells, first highlight the cells you want to join, and then choose the Join command.

8. **S**plit allows you to split a single cell into two or more cells.

In this lesson, you learned how to create a table and the basics of how to format the table. In the next lesson, you learn how to add WordPerfect clipart and other graphic elements to your document.

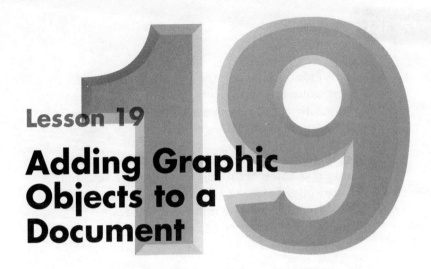

Lesson 19

Adding Graphic Objects to a Document

In this lesson, you learn how to add WordPerfect clipart and horizontal and vertical lines to your document.

Adding WordPerfect Clipart to Your Document

WordPerfect comes with several clipart images that you can add to your documents to spruce them up. For example, you can add a clipart image to a letter to create a customized letterhead or accent your newsletters with pictures. To insert a clipart image into your document, perform the following steps:

1. Move the cursor to the paragraph next to which you want the clipart image to appear. (The image will appear to the right of the paragraph, but you can move it later.)

2. Open the Graphics menu and select Retrieve Image. The Retrieve Image File dialog box appears.

3. Press F5 or click on the File List button.

4. In the Directory text box, type the path to the directory that contains the WordPerfect clipart. (This should be C:\WP60, unless you installed the clipart in a different directory during the installation process.)

5. Press Enter or click on the OK button. A list of clipart files appears. (The clipart files have the extension .WPG, which stands for WordPerfect Graphic.)

6. Highlight the name of the file you want to retrieve, and press Enter. WordPerfect inserts the selected clipart image into your document and wraps the text around it, as shown in Figure 19.1.

Graphics box

```
 File   Edit   View   Layout   Tools   Font   Graphics   Window   Help
 Marg ▼  None              ▼  1 Col ▼  Left ▼  Roman 10cpi          ▼  12pt ▼
 File Mgr  Save As  Print  Preview  Font  Grphilode TextMode Envelope Speller Grambt ik QuikFndr Tbl Edit Search
                     Contrary to Continental Drift
   Most scientists mistakenly assume that the theory of continental
   drift is fact. We must not forget that, like evolution, the
   theory is a theory, no more nor less a theory than any other.

   And that brings me to my next
   point: my theory of continental
   drift. I have examined all the
   evidence on this subject, only to
   find that no evidence proves be-
   yond the shadow of a doubt that
   continental drift is a fact. I
   have flown over the seven conti-
   nents and over several countries,
   without seeing a single continent
   drift anywhere. In addition, I
   have examined several maps,
   including the one shown here, that
   reveal the total absurdity of the
   theory. Just look at the map shown
   above. This map proves that the
   continents are not drifting at
   all. Instead, the entire globe is
 C:\DATA\WP51\FILES\CONTRAIR.DOC                    Doc 1 Pg 1 Ln 1" Pos 1"
```

Clipart image

Figure 19.1   WordPerfect inserts the clipart image into your document.

Graphics boxes. Whenever you insert an image into your document, the image is inserted in a *graphics box*. Each box is assigned a number that is used to refer to the image.

Resizing and Moving the Clipart Image with Your Mouse

When you insert a clipart image into your document, WordPerfect places the image to the right of the current paragraph and makes the image the default size, which may be too big or too small for your use. The quickest way to move or resize the image is to use the mouse, as follows:

1. Move the mouse pointer anywhere on top of the clipart image and click the left mouse button. Handles appear around the image, as shown in Figure 19.2.

2. To change the size of the image, move the mouse pointer over one of the handles, hold down the left mouse button, and drag the handle until the dotted outline of the image is the desired size and dimensions. (Drag a side handle to change one dimension at a time; drag a corner handle to change two dimensions.)

3. To move the image, move the mouse pointer anywhere over the image (except on a handle), hold down the left mouse button, and drag the image where you want it. Release the mouse button. (If you move the image, WordPerfect automatically rewraps the text around the graphics box.)

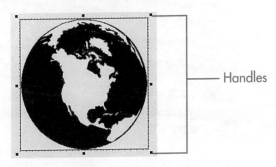

Handles

Figure 19.2 When you click on an image, handles surround it.

Editing a Graphic Image

If you do not have a mouse, or if you want to change other aspects of the clipart image, you can display the Edit Graphics Box dialog box, as shown in Figure 19.3. To display the Edit Graphics Box dialog box, perform the following steps:

1. Press Alt+F9 or open the Graphics menu.

2. Select Graphics Boxes, and then select Edit. The Select Box to Edit dialog box appears, prompting you to specify which graphics box you want to edit.

3. Select 1. Document Box Number, type the number of the graphics box you want to edit, press Enter, and select Edit Box. The Edit Graphics Box dialog box for the specified graphics box appears.

4. Enter any desired changes, and then choose OK.

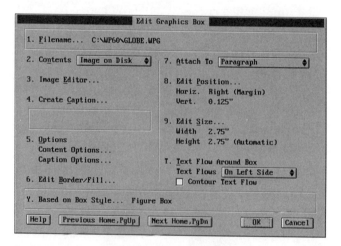

Figure 19.3 The Edit Graphics Box dialog box gives you complete control over the appearance, location, and dimensions of the image.

More Information About the Options.
For more information about any of the options in
the Edit Graphics Box dialog box, select the
option and then press the F1 key.

Prevent distortion. When resizing a graphics
box, specify the size for only one dimension
(length *or* height) and let WordPerfect determine
the other dimension. This keeps the relative
dimensions of the object consistent.

Adding Lines to Your Document

In addition to clipart, you can accent your documents by
adding vertical (up and down) or horizontal (left to right)
lines to your document. To add a line to your document,
perform the following steps:

1. Move the cursor where you want the line to appear.

2. Press Alt+F9 or open the Graphics menu.

3. Choose Graphics Lines and then Create. The Create
   Graphics Line dialog box appears, as shown in
   Figure 19.4.

4. To create a vertical line, choose 1. Line Orientation,
   and select Vertical. (If you do not specify an orientation, WordPerfect creates a horizontal line.)

5. To change the position of the line in relation to the
   left and right margins, select 2. Horizontal Position
   and select your preference.

6. To change the position of the line in relation to the
   top and bottom margins, select 3. Vertical Position

and select your preference. (The **Baseline** setting places the line at the current cursor position, where the text would normally rest.)

7. To change the thickness of the line, choose 4. Thickness, and enter a setting.

8. If you did not set the vertical or horizontal position to Full, you can choose 5. Length and specify a length for the line.

9. To specify a line style for the line (for example, double-line or dashed-line), select 6. Line Style, and choose the type of line you want to create.

10. Press Enter or click on OK to create the line.

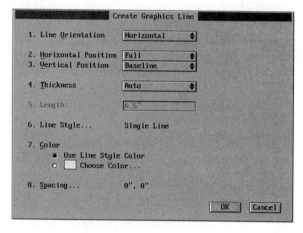

Figure 19.4 The Create Graphics Line dialog box allows you to create a vertical or horizontal line.

Moving and Resizing a Line

Chances are the line you just placed in your document is not the exact size or in the exact place where you want it. To resize or move the line, you can use your mouse or display the Edit Graphics Line dialog box, which looks a lot like the Create Graphics Line dialog box. To use the mouse, perform the following steps:

1. Move the tip of the mouse pointer until it touches any part of the line, and click the left mouse button. Handles appear around the line.

2. To make the line shorter or longer, drag one of the end handles.

3. To make the line wider or narrower, drag one of the handles that is in the middle of the line.

4. To move the line, drag any part of the line except a handle.

To move or resize a line using the Edit Graphics Line dialog box, perform the following steps:

1. Press Alt+F9 or open the Graphics menu.

2. Select Graphics Lines and then Edit.

3. Choose 1. Graphics Line Number, type the number of the graphics line you want to edit, and press Enter. You can also use the Next or Previous options if you are unsure of the line's number.

4. Press Enter or select Edit Line. The Edit Graphics Line dialog box appears for the specified line.

5. Change any of the settings, as explained for creating the line, and then select the OK button.

In this lesson, you learned how to add clipart and graphics lines to your document and how to manipulate graphics elements. In the next lesson, you learn how to add headers and footers to your documents.

Lesson 20
Adding Headers and Footers

In this lesson, you learn how to add text that appears at the top or bottom of every page in your document.

What Are Headers and Footers?

A header is text that appears at the top of every page of a document. For example, when creating this book, I used a header that indicated the title of the book, the chapter number, the page number, and the date on which I printed the chapter. A footer is just like a header, except that a footer appears at the bottom of every page.

Creating a Header or Footer

To create a header or footer, take these steps:

1. Move the cursor to the first page on which you want the header or footer to appear. The header or footer will appear on this and all following pages.

2. Press Shift+F8 or open the Layout menu.

3. Select Header/Footer/Watermark. The Header/Footer/Watermark dialog box appears.

4. Select 1. Headers or 2. Footers.

5. Select 1. Header A or 1. Footer A. You can create up to two headers (A and B) and two footers (A and

B). A dialog box appears, asking you to specify on which pages you want the header or footer to appear.

6. Select 1. All Pages, 2. Even Pages, or 3. Odd Pages.

7. Select Create. The Header or Footer edit screen appears. This screen looks like the normal edit screen, except the status line indicates that you are creating a header or footer.

8. Type the text that you want to use for the header or footer. (You can type up to one page of text, but usually you type only one or two lines.)

9. To have WordPerfect insert the page number in the header or footer, move the cursor where you want the page number to be inserted, and press Ctrl+P. The current page number appears.

10. To have WordPerfect insert the date, press Shift+F5 and select 1. Date Text or 2. Date Code (see Figure 20.1). Date Text inserts today's date as kept by your computer. Date Code inserts the current date; if you print the document tomorrow, tomorrow's date is inserted.

11. When you finish entering your header or footer, press F7 to exit the screen.

Viewing a header or footer. Headers and footers are not displayed on the edit screen. To view a header or footer, press Shift+F7 or open the File menu, and select Print Preview. The header or footer will also appear when you print the document. For more information about previewing a document, refer to Lesson 7.

This line shows the header text as it will
appear at the top of page 1.

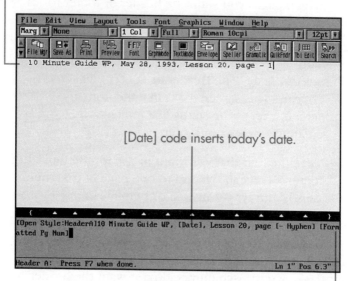

[Date] code inserts today's date.

[Formatted Pg Num] code inserts the
correct page number for each page.

Figure 20.1 A sample header complete with date and page
number (Reveal Codes is turned on).

Formatting text. You can format header and
footer text as you normally would, changing the
font size or adding attributes such as bold and
italic. You can even press Alt+F3 to display the
Reveal Codes screen in order to see the formatting codes
you have applied.

Editing a Header or Footer

If you decide to change your header or footer later, you can
edit it by performing the following steps:

1. Press Shift+F8 or open the Layout menu.

2. Select Header/Footer/Watermark. The Header/
Footer/Watermark dialog box appears.

3. Select 1. Headers or 2. Footers.

4. Select the header or footer you want to edit.

5. Select Edit. The Header or Footer edit screen appears, showing you the text you previously typed for this header or footer.

6. Edit the header or footer as you would edit any text.

7. When you finish editing your header or footer, press F7 to exit the screen.

Turning Off a Header or Footer

Unless you specify otherwise, WordPerfect sets the header or footer on all the pages, the odd pages, or the even pages, according to your initial instructions. However, you may have a title page on which you do not want the header or footer to appear. To turn a header or footer off for a single page, perform the following steps:

1. Move the cursor to the page for which you want to turn the header or footer off.

2. Press Shift+F8 or open the Layout menu.

3. Select Header/Footer/Watermark. The Header/Footer/Watermark dialog box appears.

4. Select 1. Headers or 2. Footers.

5. Select the header or footer you want to turn off.

6. Select Off. The specified header or footer will not appear on the current page.

In this lesson, you learned how to add headers and footers to a document and how to turn headers and footers off for individual pages. In the next lesson, you learn how to control the page divisions in a document and another way to number pages.

Lesson 21

Adding Page Breaks and Page Numbers

In this lesson, you learn how to force a page division and have WordPerfect automatically number the pages in your document.

Forcing a Page Break

As you type a document, WordPerfect automatically divides the document into pages based on the default page length and margin settings or on the settings you entered. Whenever WordPerfect determines that a new page should start, WordPerfect inserts a [SPg] code, which indicates a *soft page break*. WordPerfect also displays a horizontal line showing the page break on-screen. If you add or delete text before the [SPg] code, WordPerfect moves the code as needed to redivide the text into pages.

Sometimes you want to divide the text into pages yourself. For example, you may create a large table that you want to appear on a page by itself. In such a case, you can insert a *hard page break* in the document by performing the following steps:

1. Move the cursor where you want to create a page break.

2. Press Ctrl+Enter. WordPerfect inserts a [HPg] code at the cursor position and displays the page break as a double horizontal line (see Figure 21.1).

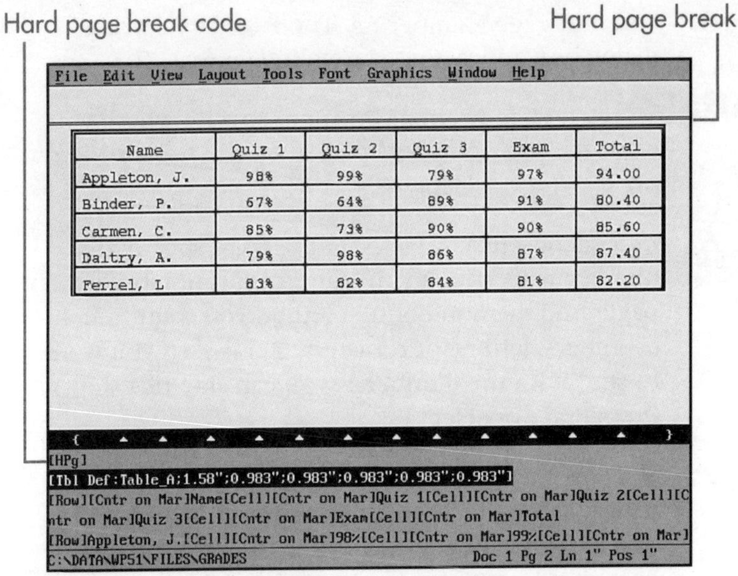

Hard page break code   Hard page break

Figure 21.1 A hard page break appears as a double horizontal line.

To remove a hard page break, press Alt+F3 to turn on Reveal Codes, highlight the [HPg] code, and press Del.

Telling WordPerfect to Number the Pages

In Lesson 20, you learned how to add headers and footers to your document and how to insert a code in a header or footer that automatically inserts the correct page number. However, WordPerfect offers an easier way to number pages, as explained in the following steps:

1. Press Home,Home,↑ to move the cursor to the top of the document.

2. Press Shift+F8 or open the Layout menu.

3. Select Page. The Page Format dialog box appears.

4. Select 1. Page Numbering. The Page Numbering dialog box appears, as shown in Figure 21.2.

5. Select 1. Page Number Position, specify where you want the page numbers placed on the page, and press Enter or select OK.

6. If needed, select 2. Page Number and specify the number with which you want to start numbering pages and the numbering method you want to use (numbers, letters, or roman numerals). (If you want to start with the number 1, you can skip this step.) Press Enter or select OK.

7. Select 6. Page Number Format, and type any text that you want to appear before the page number (for example, Page-). The [page #] code inserts the correct page numbers in your document.

8. Press Enter or click on the OK button. You are returned to the Page Format dialog box.

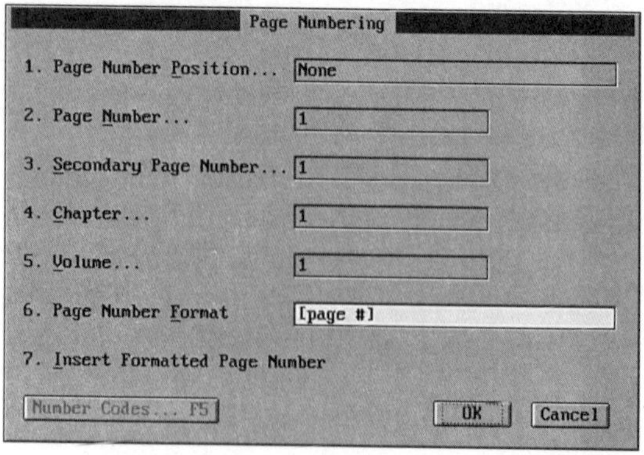

Figure 21.2   The Page Numbering dialog box prompts you to specify your page number preferences.

9. Press Enter or click on the OK button, and then click on the Close button if the Format dialog box is displayed. You are returned to the edit screen, and the [Pg Num Pos] code is inserted at the top of the document.

> **What about the other options?** The Page Numbering dialog box contains several advanced options for inserting a secondary page number, chapter number, and volume number. These options are designed for use with master documents (documents which combine two or more documents), and are not covered in this book.

In this lesson, you learned how to force a page break in a document and how to use WordPerfect's page numbering feature. In the next lesson, you learn how to work with two or more documents in separate windows.

Lesson 22

Working with Multiple Documents

In this lesson, you learn how to open two or more documents in separate windows and switch from one document to the other.

It is often useful to work with two or more documents at the same time. For example, say you are writing a letter to follow up on a letter you have previously sent. You can open the first letter in one window and switch to that letter as needed while writing your follow-up letter in another window. You can even copy text (including the inside address) from the old letter to the new one.

Opening Another Document

To open a document, you perform the same steps you perform in Lesson 6:

1. Press Shift+F10 or open the File menu and select Open. The Open Document dialog box appears.

2. Type the drive letter, path, and name of the file you want to open.

3. Press Enter or click on the OK button. WordPerfect opens a new window covering the previous window (don't worry, the previous window is still there) and retrieves the specified document into the window.

As shown in Figure 22.1, the status line shows the number of the current document.

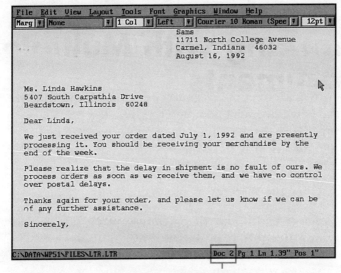

File Edit View Layout Tools Font Graphics Window Help
Marg ▼ None   ▼ 1 Col ▼ Left ▼ Courier 10 Roman (Spee ▼ 12pt ▼

                              Sams
                              11711 North College Avenue
                              Carmel, Indiana 46032
                              August 16, 1992

Ms. Linda Hawkins
5407 South Carpathia Drive
Beardstown, Illinois 60248

Dear Linda,

We just received your order dated July 1, 1992 and are presently
processing it. You should be receiving your merchandise by the
end of the week.

Please realize that the delay in shipment is no fault of ours. We
process orders as soon as we receive them, and we have no control
over postal delays.

Thanks again for your order, and please let us know if we can be
of any further assistance.

Sincerely,

C:\DATA\WP51\FILES\LTR.LTR   Doc 2 Pg 1 Ln 1.39" Pos 1"

WordPerfect displays the number of the active document.

Figure 22.1   Look at the status line to determine which document you are working on.

Switching Between Documents

Once you have two or more documents opened, you can switch from one document to the other in any of the following ways:

- To switch back and forth between the newly opened document and the previous document, press Shift+F3 or open the Window menu and select Switch.

- To switch to the previous document, open the Window menu and select Previous.

- To switch to the next document, open the Window menu and select Next or press Ctrl+Y.

- To switch to a specific document, press F3 or open the Window menu and select Switch To. The Switch To Document dialog box appears. Type the number of the document you want to switch to.

Displaying Multiple Documents on One Screen

When WordPerfect opens another document, the window for the new document completely covers the previous document. To display all the documents, you can have WordPerfect display the windows *tiled* (side-by-side) or *cascading* (overlapping), as follows:

1. Open the Window menu.

2. Select Tile to have the windows appear side-by-side or Cascade to have the windows overlap.

> **Switching windows.** When windows are tiled or cascaded, you can use the same techniques explained earlier to switch from one window to another. In addition, if you have a mouse, you can switch windows simply by clicking anywhere inside the desired window.

Minimizing and Maximizing Windows

If you have several windows open at once, each window may be too small to do any real work inside it. You can *maximize* the active window to make it take up the entire screen by performing the following steps:

1. Switch to the window you want to maximize.

2. Open the Window menu and select Maximize. The window expands to take up the full screen.

When you finish working in a window, you may want to *minimize* it so that it takes up less screen space and you can get at the other windows. To minimize a window, perform these steps:

1. Switch to the window you want to minimize.

2. Open the Window menu and select Minimize. The window shrinks.

> **The Frame option.** You may have noticed that the **W**indow menu contains another option called **F**rame. This option turns the frame around a window on if the window is maximized. The frame contains several buttons that are useful for controlling windows if you have a mouse, as discussed later in this lesson.

Closing a Document Window

When you finish working with a document, you should close the document to free up your computer's memory for other tasks. To close a document window, perform the following steps:

1. Switch to the document window you want to close.

2. Open the File menu and select Close. If you made any changes to the file since the last time you saved it, a dialog box appears asking if you want to save your changes. If you have not changed the file, WordPerfect closes the window.

3. If a dialog box appears, select the desired option.

Once you have closed all the windows you do not want to work in, you can maximize the remaining window.

Controlling Windows with a Mouse

If you have a mouse, you can use it to move, maximize, minimize, and close document windows simply by clicking and dragging parts of the window. Figure 22.2 illustrates the various mouse techniques you can use to control windows.

Click here to exit the document. (This is the same as the Exit command on the File menu.)

Click here to maximize window.

Click here to minimize window.

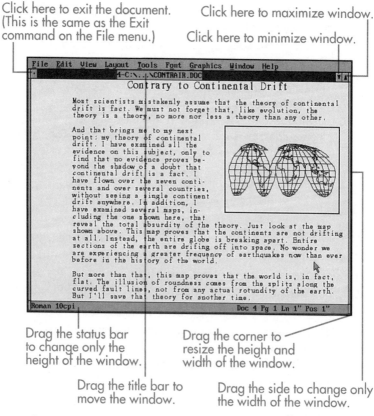

Drag the status bar to change only the height of the window.

Drag the corner to resize the height and width of the window.

Drag the title bar to move the window.

Drag the side to change only the width of the window.

Figure 22.2 You can control windows more easily with a mouse.

Copying or Moving Text Between Documents

When you have two documents open, it is easy to copy or move text from one document to the other. Perform the following steps:

1. Open the two documents you want to work with.

2. Switch to the document from which you want to copy the text.

3. Highlight the text you want to copy, as explained in Lesson 8.

4. To copy text, press Ctrl+C or open the Edit menu and select Copy. To move text, press Ctrl+X or open the Edit menu and select Cut.

5. Switch to the document into which you want to insert the text, and move the cursor where you want the text inserted.

6. Press Ctrl+V or open the Edit menu and select Paste. The text is inserted at the cursor position.

In this lesson, you learned how to work with two or more documents and how to cut, copy, and paste text from one document to another. In the next lesson, you learn how to use WordPerfect's File Manager to take more control over your files.

Lesson 23

Managing Files in WordPerfect

In this lesson, you learn how to use WordPerfect's File Manager to view, open, copy, and print files from a file list.

WordPerfect's File Manager allows you to manage all your disks, directories, and files without leaving WordPerfect and without having to rely on DOS's clumsy file management tools. With File Manager, you simply select the files you want to work with from a list, and then enter the command to view, open, copy, or print the files.

Viewing a List of Files in the File Manager

Before you can use the File Manager to work with your files, you must open the File Manager. Take the following steps:

1. Press F5 or open the File menu and select File Manager. The Specify File Manager List dialog box appears.

2. Type a path to the directory where you think the file is located, or press F8 to view the directory tree, and then select a directory.

3. Press Enter or click on the OK button. The File Manager appears, as shown in Figure 23.1.

Select Parent to move up in the directory tree.

```
                        ┌──────────────── File Manager ────────────────┐
 Directory:  C:\DATA\TMGWP6\*.*                          04-21-93   11:32a
 ┌─Sort by: Filename ────────────────────────┐
 │   .    Current     <Dir>                 ↑ │  1. Open into New Document
 │   ..   Parent      <Dir>                   │  2. Retrieve into Current Doc
 │  01TMWP6 .BAK    7,680  03-31-93 04:27p    │  3. Look...
 │  01TMWP6 .DOC    8,192  04-05-93 02:06p    │
 │  02TMWP6 .BAK    9,216  04-05-93 02:09p    │  4. Copy...
 │  02TMWP6 .DOC    9,216  04-05-93 02:09p    │  5. Move/Rename...
 │  03TMWP6 .BAK    5,120  04-01-93 12:28p    │  6. Delete
 │  03TMWP6 .DOC    5,120  04-05-93 02:57p    │  7. Print...
 │  03TMWP6 .WP5    4,566  03-31-93 01:05p    │  8. Print List
 │  03TMWP6 .WPF    7,436  03-26-93 03:43p    │
 │  04TMWP6 .BAK    7,680  04-05-93 02:17p    │  9. Sort by...
 │  04TMWP6 .DOC    7,680  04-05-93 02:57p    │  H. Change Default Dir...
 │  04TMWP6 .WP5    5,386  03-31-93 01:06p    │  U. Current Dir... F5
 │  04TMWP6 .WPF    7,621  03-26-93 03:41p    │  F. Find...
 │  05TMWP6 .BAK    6,144  04-05-93 02:18p    │  E. Search... F2
 │  05TMWP6 .DOC    6,144  04-05-93 02:57p    │  N. Name Search
 │  05TMWP6 .WP5    4,418  03-31-93 01:06p    │
 │  05TMWP6 .WPF    7,031  03-29-93 08:41a    │  * (Un)mark
 │  06TMWP6 .BAK   12,288  04-05-93 04:32p  ↓ │  Home,* (Un)mark All
 ├─Files:     98 ──── Marked:       0 ────────┤
   Free:   7,139,328  Used:   756,468            [Setup... Shft+F1]  [Close]
```

Files in the current directory   Commands

Figure 23.1 The File Manager shows a list of subdirectories and files contained in the specified directory.

The File Manager initially displays the contents of the specified directory. However, you can change to a different directory by performing these steps:

1. To move to a subdirectory of the current directory, highlight the subdirectory and press Enter, or double-click on the subdirectory name.

2. To move up one level in the directory tree, highlight .. Parent <Dir> and press Enter, or double-click on it with your mouse. A list of subdirectories and files in the selected directory appears.

Viewing the Contents of a File

Sometimes you may be unsure whether the document in the list is the one you want to open. In such cases, it is useful to view the contents of the file before opening it. To view the contents of a file, perform the following steps:

1. Use the arrow keys to highlight the name of the file you want to look at, or click on the name with your mouse.

2. Select 3. Look. The document appears on-screen.

3. To view the next document in the list, select 1. Next. To look at the previous document, select 2. Previous.

4. To scroll through the document, select Scroll. WordPerfect scrolls slowly to the end of the document or until you select Scroll again. (If you have a mouse, you can use the scroll bar.)

5. When you are finished viewing the file, press Esc to return to the File Manager, or select 3. Open to open the document.

Copying text. You can copy text from the document to the clipboard without opening the document. Move the cursor to the beginning or end of the block you want to copy, press Alt+F4, and move the cursor to the opposite end of the block. Press Ctrl+F1, and then choose 1. Save Block to Clipboard or 2. Append Block to Clipboard. You can then paste the block in an open document.

Marking Files in the File List

If you want to work with only one file in the file list, you can specify the desired file simply by using the arrow keys or mouse to highlight it. To work with two or more files (for example, to open three files at once), you must first mark the files, as follows:

1. Use the arrow keys to highlight the file you want to mark, or click on the file with your mouse.

2. Press the spacebar or select * (Un)mark. An asterisk appears to the left of the filename, showing that the file is marked.

3. To unmark a file, repeat steps 1 and 2.

> **Mark or unmark all files.** To mark or unmark all files in the list, press Home,* or click on (Un)mark All.

Opening or Retrieving a File

You can open or retrieve one or more files by entering the appropriate command in the File Manager. Keep in mind that the **O**pen command retrieves the document into a new window, whereas the **R**etrieve command opens the document into the current document. If you open more than one document, each document is opened in a separate window. If you retrieve more than one document, all the documents are opened in the same window. To open or retrieve documents, perform the following steps:

1. Highlight the document or mark the documents you want to open or retrieve.

2. Select 1. Open into New Document or 2. Retrieve into Current Doc. The document(s) is opened or retrieved as specified.

Copying Files

You often need to create copies of your documents for various purposes. For example, you may want to copy files from your hard disk to a floppy disk to share with a friend or colleague or to act as backup files in case the originals get deleted or damaged. Or, you may want to create a copy of a file so you can edit it without changing the original. Whatever the reason, you can easily copy files by performing the following steps:

1. Highlight the file or mark the files you want to copy.

2. Select 4. Copy. If you marked more than one file, a confirmation box appears; select Yes. A dialog box appears, prompting you to specify where you want the file(s) copied to (see Figure 23.2).

3. To copy the file(s) to a different drive or directory, type a path to the directory, or press F8 and select the directory from the directory tree.

   If you select only one file and wish to create an exact copy of the file in the same directory, type a new name for the copy. (You cannot have two files with the same name in the same directory.)

4. Press Enter or click on the OK button. WordPerfect copies the file(s).

Deleting Files

If you have documents that you never use, you may want to delete them from your hard disk in order to free up valuable disk space. Be careful, however; when you delete files, you cannot recover them using WordPerfect. To delete one or more files, take the following steps:

1. Highlight the file you want to delete, or mark the files.

2. Choose 6. Delete. A dialog box appears, asking you to confirm the deletion.

3. Select Yes to confirm the deletion or press Enter to select No and cancel the deletion. If you marked one or more files, another dialog box appears, to

make sure you really really want to delete the files.
(If you just highlighted a filename, no confirmation
box appears.)

4. Select Yes to confirm again or Enter to just say No.
The marked files are deleted.

These marked files will be copied.

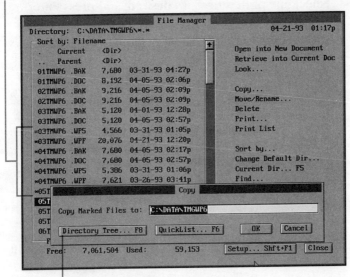

This button displays a directory
tree for the current disk drive.

Figure 23.2 Type a path to the directory where you want
the file(s) copied.

Printing Files

Although you can print multiple files by opening each file
and selecting the Print command from the File menu, sometimes it may be easier to print the files from the File Manager. Here's how:

1. Highlight the file you want to print, or mark the
files.

2. Select 7. Print. If you marked one or more files, a dialog box appears asking if you really want to print the files.

3. Select Yes. The Print Multiple Pages dialog box appears, prompting you to enter any specifics about the print job.

4. Select any preferences, as desired, and press Enter or click on the OK button. WordPerfect starts printing the files.

> **Canceling the print job.** If you change your mind about printing the files, or something goes wrong during the printing operation, exit the File Manager and then stop or cancel the print jobs, as explained in Lesson 7. Here's a quick review: Press Shift+F7, select 6. Control Printer, select 4. (Un)mark All, and select Stop.

In this lesson, you learned how to use WordPerfect's File Manager to view, open, retrieve, copy, delete, and print files. This is the last lesson in this book. The appendix that follows contains a list of WordPerfect's hidden formatting codes and descriptions of what each one does.

Appendix A

WordPerfect Formatting Codes

Following are a list of common formatting codes that WordPerfect uses to control the look and layout of your document. Refer to Lesson 12 to learn how to display and work with codes.

Code	What It Does
[-Hyphen]	Indicates a hyphen that you have added by pressing the hyphen key
[-Soft Hyphen]	Indicates a hyphen that WordPerfect has added if you turned the automatic hyphenation feature on
[Back Tab]	Returns the cursor to the previous tab stop
[Bold Off]	Turns bold off
[Bold On]	Turns bold on
[Bot Mar]	Sets the bottom margin
[Box]	Controls various aspects of graphics boxes, including the numbering method (there are several [Box] codes)
[Cntr Cur Pg]	Centers text vertically on the current page
[Cntr on Mar]	Centers a line of text between the left and right margins
[Cntr Pgs]	Centers text vertically on pages
[CNTR TAB]	Centers text on a tab stop
[Date]	Inserts today's date as kept by your computer's clock

continues

Code	What It Does
[Dbl Und Off]	Turns double-underlining off
[Dbl Und On]	Turns double-underlining on
[DEC TAB]	Aligns text on a decimal point at a tab stop
[Ext Large Off]	Turns extra large text off
[Ext Large On]	Turns extra large text on
[Fine Off]	Turns fine text off
[Fine On]	Turns fine text on
[Flsh Rgt]	Aligns the end of each line of text against the right margin
[Font]	Specifies the type size and style for the text
[Footer]	Inserts a footer that appears at the bottom of each document page
[Header]	Inserts a header that appears at the top of each document page
[HPg]	Tells WordPerfect to start a new page
[HRt]	Indicates the end of a paragraph
[Italc Off]	Turns italicizing off
[Italc On]	Turns italicizing on
[Just:Cntr]	Centers the text between the margins
[Just:Full]	Extends text from the left to right margins
[Just:Right]	Places the right side of each line of text against the right margin
[Large Off]	Turns large text off
[Large On]	Turns large text on
[Lft Indent]	Indents the entire left side of a paragraph to the next tab stop
[Lft Indent] [Back Tab]	Creates a hanging indent (as for a bulleted or numbered list)

Code	What It Does
[Lft Mar]	Sets the left margin
[Lft Tab]	Aligns the left end of a line against a tab stop setting
[Lft/Rgt Indent]	Indents text from both the left and right margins
[Ln Height]	Sets the line height
[Ln Spacing]	Sets the line spacing (single, double, triple, etc.)
[Outln Off]	Turns the outline feature off
[Outln On]	Turns the outline feature on
[Paper Sz/Typ]	Enters the settings for the paper size and type
[Pg Num]	Specifies the location and appearance of page numbers for the automatic page numbering feature (there are several [Pg Num] codes)
[Redln Off]	Turns redlining off
[Redln On]	Turns redlining on
[Rgt Mar]	Sets the right margin
[Rgt Tab]	Aligns the right side of a line of text against a tab stop
[Shadw Off]	Turns character shadowing off
[Shadw On]	Turns character shadowing on
[Small Off]	Turns small text off
[Small On]	Turns small text on
[Sm Cap Off]	Turns small capitalization off
[Sm Cap On]	Turns small capitalization on
[SRt]	Indicates the end of a line in a paragraph
[StkOut Off]	Turns strikeout off
[StkOut On]	Turns strikeout on

continues

Code	What It Does
[Supress]	Prevents a header or footer from being printed on a page
[Tab]	Aligns the left end of a line of text against a tab stop
[Tab Set]	Inserts settings that control the positions and types of tab stops
[Tbl Def]	Defines the overall structure and appearance of a table
[Tbl Off]	Turns a table off, returning to normal text
[Top Mar]	Sets the top margin
[Und Off]	Turns underlining off
[Und On]	Turns underlining on
[Very Large Off]	Turns very large text off
[Very Large On]	Turns very large text on
[Watermark]	Inserts a watermark on the page

Index

Help menu, 3-5
hidden codes, *see* codes
horizontal
    blinking line, 2
    graphic lines, 109-110
    orientation (landscape),
        79
    scroll bars, 21-23

I-J

indenting text, 77-78
    paragraphs, 18
initial fonts, 63
Insert mode, 24

joining cells, 104
justification, 75-77

K

keys
    Backspace, 26
    cursor-movement, 20
    Del, 26
    shortcut, *see* shortcut keys
    Tab, 18, 25, 68

L

landscape (horizontal)
    orientation, 79
left
    justification, 75-76
    tab stops, 69-70
line spacing, 73-75
lines
    centering or right-
        justifying, 77

graphic
    adding to documents,
        109-110
    moving or resizing,
        110-111
    in cells, 103
list boxes, 11
location, paper, 79

M

macros, 4
margins, 80-83
marking files, 128-129
maximizing document
    windows, 122-123
memory, 1
menu bar, 2
    displaying, 9
menus, 7-8
    closing without selecting
        commands, 10
    Font, 55-57
    Help, 3-5
    selecting commands, 7-10
messages, Bad command or
    filename, 2
minimizing document
    windows, 122-123
modes
    Graphics, 14-15
    Insert, 24
    Text, 14
    Typeover, 24-25
mouse
    navigating
        dialog boxes, 12
        documents, 21